Stoic Inspirations

EPICTETUS' DISCOURES BOOK 5

STOICISM IN PLAIN ENGLISH

Dr Chuck Chakrapani

The Stoic Gym Publications

Stoic Gym Publications
www.thestoicgym.com

Ordering Information:
Quantity sales. Special discounts are available on quantity purchases by corporations, associations, and others. For details, contact the "Special Sales Department" at the address above.

Stoic Foundations/Chuck Chakrapani. —1st ed.
ISBN: **9780920219409**

17 18 19 20 21 22 23 24 25 26   1 2 3 4 5 6 7 8 9 0

Contents

Stoic Inspirations

Some new material, but mostly a summary

This book contains a biography of Epictetus, the sayings of Epictetus (also called *Fragments,* some of which are not in any of the precious four books in this series) and two summaries of the works of Epictetus. The two summaries – *Enchiridion* and the Golden Sayings – draw heavily from *Discourses. Enchiridion* and the Golden Sayings themselves have some overlap between them, This is not necessarily a bad thing when one tries to internalize the profound truths of Stoic thoughts and be inspired by them.

Consequently the primary purpose of this book is to reinforce what we have already learned in the previous four books. It can also be an inspiring reminder of the principles learned earlier and lead us to a life of serenity, happiness and freedom..

Here's an outline of what is in this book:

1

Contents of this book

This book has four parts.

1. The man who was Epictetus

The opening chapter of the book outlines the life and times of Epictetus, whose teachings we have explored in the previous four books in this series and continue to explore in this book.

2. Fragments (Epictetus, as quoted by others)

The second chapter is a collection of Epictetus' sayings as quoted by others. They are not too numerous, but the collection does contain quotes not found in *Discourses*. Although a number of quotes have been attributed to Epictetus our collection is limited to what has been confined to what has been judged to be authentic or near-authentic quotes.

3. The golden sayings of Epictetus

These are extracts from Epictetus' works, mostly from *Discourses* and *Fragments*. The extracts were initially translated and compiled by Hastings Crossley during the early 20th Century. Although it is a good summary of Epictetus' teachings, it is longer than the other summary *Enchiridion*, compiled by Arrian. Many passages in The Golden Sayings have a devotional slant.

4. *Enchiridion* (The Handbook)

Enchiridion or The Handbook is a compilation of Epictetus' teachings. It is short and is one of the best-known books on Stoicism. (It is also available as a separate volume, published by The Stoic Gym.)

A note on the plain English version

Like the other books in this series, this is a plain English version. This means I have used modern English as well as simple word and sentences. I have also tried to use non-sexist language and used titles, subtitles, and comments to make it easy for the contemporary reader. Occasionally, I have even shortened some passages.

There is some trade-off, however, resulting in differences between this version and literal translations. While they may mean the same thing, if you need the literal translation for scholarly purposes, you should consult other sources that are widely available.

PART 1

The Man
Who Was Epictetus

Anthony and Cleopatra vs. Octavian: The founding of Nicopolis

In 31 BCE, in the Ionian Sea near Berenkea, the navy of Anthony and Cleopatra fought fiercely that of Octavian. In this major naval battle, Octavian defeated Anthony and Cleopatra.

To celebrate his success, Octavian built the city of Nicopolis (Victory City). It was a flourishing city and at its peak had a population of 150,000. (The ruins of the city now stands in the outskirts of the modern city of Preveza in Greece.)

A lame philosopher arrives

Some 50 or so years later, a lame philosopher arrived there after being expelled from Rome by Emperor Domitian. He founded a philosophy school there and began teaching well to do Romans and others on how to flourish in life. He lived there until his death over forty years afterwards.

The exiled philosopher achieved fame while he was still alive. Many prominent people, including the Emperor of the Roman Empire, were influenced by his teachings.

His influence continues to this day, some two thousand years afterwards. Among other things, his teachings influenced three schools of modern psychotherapy and provided guidance to people from different walks of life.

- Who was he?
- What was his name?
- When was he born?
- When did he die?
- Was he really lame?
- How did he become lame?

It is said that his name was Epictetus, he was born in 55 CE and died in 135 CE. He became lame because, when he was a slave, his master broke his leg for fun. While these "facts" are not very often challenged, we really don't know if any of it is true.

What do we know about this philosopher, whom we call Epictetus? The next section answers some questions about Epictetus' life.

The Life of Epictetus: What we know

Here is what we know for sure about Epictetus.

When was he born?

Sometime between 50-60 CE, often assumed to be 55 CE. He was of Greek parentage.

Where was he born?

Probably in Hierapolis (currently known as Pamukkale), Phrygia. It was a major Greco-Roman city situated in modern day Turkey, about 170 kilometres east of Ephesus, connected by road.

How did he become a slave?

We can't be sure, but the generally accepted version is that his mother was a slave and, when he was born, he was already a slave.

When did he come to Rome?

When he was about five years old.

What was his real name?

We are not sure.

Why not?

'Epictetus' means 'acquired.' We don't know whether it was his real name or people just called him that. We are not even sure if he was even named by his mother.

Who acquired him?

The person who acquired him was himself a former slave called Epaphroditus who, after he was freed, rose to the position of secretary to Nero.

Was he really lame, as they say?

There are many unconfirmed accounts that Epictetus leg had been broken by either Epaphroditus or the first owner of

Epictetus. But it is as likely he had knee arthritis as he got older.

How did Epictetus become a Stoic?

Even as a very young person, Epictetus showed promise. So his master sent him to study under the famous Stoic teacher Musonius Rufus.

Why would a slave be sent to study philosophy?

It is said that in those days it was not uncommon for slave-owners to be proud of their slave's abilities. So it may well be that the master sent Epictetus to study philosophy so the master could proclaim that one of his slaves was a philosopher. Epictetus showed such promise at an early age, that Epaphroditus sent him to study with Musonius. But this is just speculation.

When was Epictetus freed?

Most likely, after Nero died in in 68 CE. (Epaphroditus again became a secretary to the emperor when Domitian became the emperor in 81 CE.)

Where did Epictetus get his students from?

After Epictetus was freed, he began teaching immediately in Rome presumably with the backing of Musonius Rufus, who was famous as a Stoic philosopher.

How did Epictetus end up in Nicopolis?

Sometime between 89 and 95 CE (mostly likely 89 CE), Domitian banished all philosophers not only from Rome, which was more common, but from Italy as well. So Epictetus sailed to Greece (perhaps because he himself was of Greek origin) and settled in Nicopolis.

Who were his students?

By the time he was banished, he was probably in his mid-thirties and early forties with a well-established reputation as a Stoic philosopher. So he attracted a number of well-to-do people from Rome, which included people like Arrian, who transcribed Epictetus' *Discourses*.

How famous was Epictetus?

He was famous enough to attract full time students from Rome. There is reason to believe that Emperor Hadrian and other prominent figures visited him in Nicopolis, as can be inferred from *Discourses*. Emperor Marcus Aurelius was clearly influenced by him.

In what language did he teach?

He taught mostly in Attic Greek, although his discourses were transcribed in a common dialect, Koine Greek, by Arrian. (Arrian himself wrote in more literate Greek.)

How many books did he write?

Zero. Epictetus wrote no books. Yet we have greater access to his teachings compared to that of any other Stoic philosopher of the past. This is because he had a very distinguished students who transcribed many of Epictetus' conversations with students and visitors. *Discourses* and *Enchiridion* are considered to be authentic transcripts of his talks. They are often referred to as the works of Epictetus rather than of the scribe, Arrian.

What was his lifestyle?

Because of his influential disciples and his fame, he could have lived a luxurious life. Instead (as far as we know) he chose to live very simply. His entire furniture consisted of a rush mat, a simple pallet [bed on the floor], a cooking vessel and an earthenware lamp (after the iron one was stolen).

Lucian ridicules a man who bought the lamp after his death, for 3,000 drachmas in hopes of becoming a philosopher by using it.

He described his life this way: "I have neither city, nor house, nor possessions, nor servants: the ground is my couch; I have no wife, no children, no shelter -- nothing but earth and sky, and one poor cloak. And what lack I yet? Am I not untouched by sorrow, by fear? am I not free?" (Discourses iii, 22)

His contemporary, Aulus Gellius, says that Epictetus also wrote this:

I Epictetus,

born a slave, and lame,

as poor as Irus,

am dear to gods.

(Source: *The Attic Nights Of Aulus Gellius*; Irus was a beggar in Homer's Odyssey.)

These self-descriptions of Epictetus were never contradicted by his contemporaries, so we may assume that he lived a very simple life.

Did he have any children?

No. However, in his old age he adopted and cared for a child who would have died otherwise. He lived with the child and a live-in maid.

Was he ever married?

We don't know for sure, but he probably did marry his live-in maid in his old age to ensure that the child he adopted had a mother.

When did he die?

Again, there is no record of his death. It is generally thought he probably died around 135 CE, when he was about 80 years old.

That, in short, is the biography of an influential philosopher whose name we are not sure of, whose years of birth and death we are not sure of, and how he became lame we are not sure of either.

Yet he is arguably the most influential of the ancient Stoic philosophers, if only because we have more complete access to his teachings than to that of any other Stoic philosopher, thanks to his illustrious student, Arrian,

---

Epictetus 'gets under our skin'

"Epictetus is a thinker we cannot forget, once we encountered him, because he gets under our skin. He provokes, he irritates, but he deals so trenchantly with life's everyday challenges that no one who knows his work can simply dismiss it as theoretically invalid or practically useless." (A.A. Long. *Epictetus: A Stoic and Socratic Guide to Life*, Oxford. 2002)

Epictetus and freedom

The concept of eudemonia is often thought of as happiness, but it more than that. The word 'flourishing' is often used to describe the concept, but it is not an everyday word. Eudemonia can be seen as a combination of freedom, happiness, and serenity. Of these, Epictetus focused most on freedom. (We can also view any of these concepts as being inclusive of the other two.)

How important was the concept of freedom to Epictetus? One his longest discourses – possibly the longest – is on freedom with 177 numbered 'paragraphs' (*Discourses* Book IV.1). According to William Oldfather, the word 'free' as an adjective and verb appears 130 times in Epictetus' writings. In relative terms that is 600% more than in the New Testament and 200% more than his contemporary Stoic, Marcus Aurelius. But the freedom he talks about is not physical freedom. It has nothing to do with the social or political meaning of the word. You can be free whether you are in prison or outside, whether you are rich or poor, whether you live under dictatorship or in a democracy.

The freedom that Epictetus talks about is psychological freedom that does not depend on what condition you see yourself in. He talks about the freedom of spirit that is totally unaffected by external circumstances. He talks about the mind that is afraid of nothing that might happen.

Why are we unfree and unhappy? Because we feel defeated by other people, by what happens to us, by what we believe, and by the condition of our body. When we feel defeated, we subject ourselves to negative emotions and surrender our freedom.

Epictetus teaches it is possible to be unconditionally free, happy and serene, if you follow some basic principles. These include:

• Understanding what is under our control and what is not
• Understanding what we control is limited to 'what is our own,' and does not include our body, property, reputation etc.

- Confining our actions to only what is under our control
- Evaluating every first impression we have of people and things to see if they are what they appear to be
- Confining our choices to only things that are in our control
- Willingness to accept whatever reality hands to us
- Understanding that good and evil come only from our thinking and actions and not from externals
- Enjoying things that are not our control, as long as we are willing to give them up with no notice, should they be taken away from us

---

Four unifying concepts

A more comprehensive account of Epictetus is given by A.A. Long (*Epictetus, A Stoic and Socratic Guide to Life*, 2002) who believes that four underlying concepts unify Epictetus' thinking.

1. *Freedom* that is entirely psychological. This is freedom that is independent of external circumstances and emotional reactions.

2. *Judgment* is what we use to experience the world. Arriving at proper judgements and thus rational conclusions is entirely within our power.

3. *Volition or will* (*prohairesis*) is what we are. We are not our bodies and don't even own them. We are our mental faculties, consciousness, judgements, goals and desires. Thus volition can be considered as the self. You can achieve freedom by transferring all your desires away from externals and to the self.

4. *Integrity* is a part of volition. It refers to how that mental disposition is related to other people.

The influence of Epictetus

The influence of Epictetus is considerable. As William Oldfather notes, Emperor Hadrian was his friend and supposed to have visited him. Emperor Marcus Aurelius was a student of his teachings. Celsus, Gellius and Lucin spoke highly of him. Galen even wrote a book defending Epictetus. Many prominent Christians recognized him. His *Enchiridion* was adopted by two different Christian ascetics as a guide to monastic life.

Stoicism went into eclipse after Emperor Justinian closed the Academy in 529 CE and that pretty much ended all philosophical schools of Rome, including Stoicism. During the 16th and the 17th Centuries, there was renewed interest in Stoicism and the works of Epictetus.

Although Stoicism was dormant until the 15th Century, *Enchiridion* had always been generally available. In 1758, Elizabeth Carter published her translation of *Discourses* in English.

In the early 21st Century, there has been a revival of Stoicism, spearheaded by the University of Exeter in England. Three forms of psychotherapy – Logo therapy, Rational Emotional Behaviour Therapy (REBT), and Cognitive Behavioural Therapy (CBT) – acknowledge the influence of Stoicism. Stoicism in these cases means the ethical precepts of Stoicism, mostly as taught by Epictetus.

Although *Discourses* are records of informal discussions (rather than of classroom lecture notes) with students and visitors, because Stoic ethics is based on a few recurring principles, we can assume *Discourses* cover all the important principles of Stoic ethics, as taught by Epictetus.

PART 2

Sayings of Epictetus (Fragments)

What are fragments?

Fragments are sayings of Epictetus as quoted by others. Although Arrian was the only person who recorded the discourses of Epictetus, he was not the only one to quote Epictetus. A number of Epictetus' quotes appear in books by others. Some of them are from Arrian, but many of them are not. Some of them could also be from Arrian's four lost books of *Discourses*.

Many such quotes or 'fragments' were compiled by the Byzantine scholar Johannes Stobaeus for his son's benefit. There were also other fragments attributed to Democritus, Isocrates, and Epictetus. Initially these collections were large. Elizabeth Carter's book contains 169 of them.

Many scholars, however, have questioned the authenticity of most quotes in such collections and challenged their validity. Like them, I don't believe any purpose is served by attributing to Epictetus things he mostly likely didn't say. In this collection, I have excluded all fragments that are most likely spurious, based on reviews by scholars such as H. Schenkl, R. Asmus and A. Elter and as reported by William A. Oldfather. The rest is divided into two groups: Fragments judged to be authentic and those that may be authentic, but cannot be confirmed one way or the other.

1. Keep your practice simple

What do I care whether everything that exists is made up of atoms, indivisibles, or fire and earth? *Isn't it enough to know the nature of good and evil, the limits of desire and aversion, and of choice and refusal? Use these as rules, get our lives in order and dismiss things that we don't understand?*

Questions that are beyond our understanding, we should ignore. It may well be that the human mind cannot grasp them. Even if you think they are perfectly understandable, what's the use of understanding them? Should we not say those who think these things are an essential part of a philosopher's knowledge are creating unwanted problems for themselves?

"So, is the commandment at Delphi 'know yourself' unnecessary too?"

"No, not that for sure."

"Well, what does it mean, then?"

"If someone said to a member of the chorus 'know yourself,' it would mean that she should pay attention to other members of the chorus and sing in harmony with them."

"Yes."

"Similarly with a soldier or a sailor. So what do you think: Is a human being created to live alone or in a community?"

"In a community."

"Who created it?"

"Nature."

"What is nature? How does it administer the universe? Does nature actually exists or not? We don't need to concern ourselves with these questions."

[*Source*: Stobaeus, *Eclogae* II.1,31. From Arrian.]

2. Appreciate what you have

If you are dissatisfied with what you have and what is given to you by fate, you are unskilled in the art of living. If you bear all this in a noble spirit and make use of all that comes your way, you deserve to be called a good person.

[*Source:* Stobaeus, *Eclogae* II.44,65.]

3. Don't resist reality

All things obey and serve the universe – the land and sea, the sun and other stars, the world's plants and animals. Our body also obeys the universe – both in sickness and in health (as the universe wishes), in youth and old age, and when passing through other changes. So it is unreasonable that our will, the only thing in our power, be the only thing to try and resist the universe, which is strong and superior to us. It has taken better advice than we could for ourselves by including us in the universe and its administration.

In any case, resistance is useless. It only leads to unnecessary struggle and it accomplishes nothing except grief and sorrow.

[*Source:* Stobaeus, *Eclogae* II.44,66.]

4. Achieving freedom, serenity, and happiness is under our control

God has put some things under our control and others not in our control. Within our control are the finest and the most important things and the thing that God himself needs for his own happiness – the ability to use external impressions. If we use them the right way, they lead us to freedom, serenity, and happiness. It is also the basis of justice, law, and restraint as well as virtue.

But God has placed all other things beyond our control. So, to be of one mind with God, we should make the same distinction and claim everything that is under our control, but surrender to the universe everything not under our control. No matter what it asks for – our children, our homeland, our body, or anything else – give it up gladly.

[*Source:* Stobaeus, *Eclogae* II.8,30, Musonius, *Fragments*

XXXVIII]

5. Don't reciprocate violence

Which one of you doesn't admire what the Spartan Lycurgus said when he was blinded in one eye by a young citizen of Sparta? People turned him over to Lycurgus for punishment, the way he saw fit. Lycurgus not only did not take revenge but actually educated the youth and made a good man out of him and presented him at the theatre. The Spartans were outraged, but Lucurgus said, 'You gave me a violent and aggressive person. I am returning him as a civilized and refined person.'

[*Source:* Stobaeus, *Eclogae* III.19,13, Musonius, *Fragments* XXXIX]

6. Conform to what is right and helpful

Above all else, this is what nature asks of us: conform and adapt our choice with what is right and helpful. [Rufus, quoted by Epictetus.]

[*Source:* Stobaeus, *Eclogae* III.20,60, Musonius, *Fragments* XL]

7. Recognize despicable people by their inability to do good

To imagine that we will be despised by others unless we harm our enemies in any way we can is a mark of very mean and ignorant people. We commonly say that one can recognize a contemptible person by their inability to do harm. It would much better to recognize them by their inability to do any good.

[*Source:* Stobaeus, *Eclogae* III.20,61, Rufus, quoted by Epictetus, Musonius, *Fragments* XL]

8. Accept the inevitable for a harmonious life

The nature of the universe was, is, and always will be the same. Things cannot happen any differently than they do now. It is not just humankind that participates in this change and transformation, but also all other living beings, and the divine; even the four elements are changed and transformed up and down [from heavier to the lighter and from lighter to the heavier]. Earth becomes water, water becomes air, air becomes fire. There is the same kind of transformation the other way around.

If you try to adapt your mind to these changes, and accept voluntarily what cannot be avoided anyway, you will live a smooth and harmonious life.

[Source: Stobaeus, *Eclogae* III.44,60, Rufus, quoted by
Epictetus, Musonius, *Fragments* 42, H]

9. Understand that impressions are deceptive

A well-known Stoic philosopher pulled out of his handbag a copy of *Discourses Book V* by Epictetus and arranged by Arrian. These writings no doubt agree with those of Zeno and Chrysippus. There, written in Greek of course, we find a passage to this effect:

The way things look to our mind are called 'impressions' by philosophers. Impressions that enter our minds have an immediate psychological impact, and they are not under our choice or voluntary control. But whether we agree (or 'assent' as philosophers call it) with the impression or not is voluntary and involves our judgment. So, when you hear a terrifying sound from the sky, or from the collapse of a building, or when a sudden news comes of some danger, or something else of that kind happens, even a wise person's mind is shaken a little. It shrinks and grows pale for a moment, not from any preconceived idea that something bad is about to happen, but because some rapid and unexamined movements prevent the mind and reasoning from functioning properly.

But, soon enough, the wise person does not give assent to this impression [that is, does not believe that something terrifying has actually happened] but rejects and dismisses it completely and sees no reason in them to be afraid.

They say this is the difference between the mind of a wise versus a foolish person: the foolish person believes that the things that initially strike the mind as horrible and terrifying are exactly what they seem to be, and so approves them by assenting. But the wise person, soon regaining her colour and composure, does not assent. She reaffirms her support of the view she always had of impressions: they are not be feared in the least. They just frighten us with a false face and terror.

[*Source*: Gellius. XIX, 1, 14-21]

---

10. Two keys to happiness:
Ability to put up with things and self-control

I have heard Favorinus say this:

The philosopher Epictetus said that most of those who practice philosophy are of the kind 'far from action, only words'. He even used a more vigorous expressions, according to Arrian, who recorded it in his books. Arrian says:

Epictetus saw someone who lost all sense of shame, whose energy is misguided, who has bad habits, who was disrespectful in speech, and who was concerned about everything except their moral character. Epictetus also noticed that such a person was also studying philosophical subjects and methods, physics, and dialectic and was beginning to inquire into many such philosophical ideas. He used to appeal in the name of gods and men, and, in the middle of this appeal, would denounce him with these words:

"Man, where are you putting these things? Look and see if the jar is clean. If you store them among your opinions, they are ruined. If they rot, they become urine or vinegar or perhaps something even worse. Surely, there is nothing more important or truer than this statement: 'The writings and teachings of philosophy, when poured into a false and corrupt person, like liquids poured into a dirty and polluted jar, are altered, changed, spoiled, and (as he himself in rather Cynic style says) become urine or something even fouler than that."

The same Epictetus, as we have heard from Favorinus, is in the habit of saying that,

"There are two vices much more important and offensive than all the others: lack of self-control and inability to put up with things. We do not put up with and bear things that we should bear and we do not keep away from pleasures and things we should keep away from."

He said:

"So, someone could hold these two words to one's heart and live by them, controlling and keeping watch over themselves, they will, for the most part, be free from wrongdoing and will live a highly peaceful life."

These two words, he used to say, are 'bear' and 'forebear'.

[*Source:* Gellius. XVII, 19]

10a. When your soul is at stake, do something quickly

Arrian also approvingly quotes this saying of Epictetus:

When the salvation of our souls with regard to our true selves are at stake, something has to be done. We don't even have to stop and think about it.

[*Source:* Arnobius. *Adverses Gentes*, 2, 78]

---

11. Be content with what is given to you

When [the King of Macedon] Archelaus sent for Socrates and said that he would make him rich, Socrates told the messenger to take back the following response:

"In Athens, four quarts of barley meal can be bought for a penny and there are plenty of springs with fresh water. If what I have is not enough, I can still manage on what I have. This makes it adequate for my purposes. Don't you know that [the famous actor] Polos didn't perform the part of Oedipus as king any more pleasingly or movingly than he played the part of Oedipus at Colonus as a beggar and wanderer? Should a man of fine character show himself worse than Polos, not performing the role assigned to him by God? Should he not imitate Odysseus, who was no less dignified in rags than his royal purple robe?"

[*Source:* Stobaeus, IV.33,28]

12. Guard yourself against passive-aggressiveness

There are some people who express themselves gently in spite of their ill-temper, appearing to be detached. But they do everything that those who are totally carried away by their anger do. Therefore, we must be on our guard against the error of such people because theirs is much worse than being boiling mad. People of the latter kind are so satisfied with their revenge, but the former hold on to their anger, like one suffering from a low-grade fever

[*Source:* Stobaeus, III.20,47]

13. Virtue is more important than property

Someone said [to Epictetus]

"But I see those who are good and excellent dying of hunger and cold."

"Don't you also see those who are not noble and good dying of luxury and pretence and vulgarity?"

"Yes, but it is shameful to depend on the support provided others."

"And who, miserable fool, is really self-sufficient - except the universe of course?"

Blaming God because the wicked were not punished, but are strong and rich, is like someone saying that the wicked who have lost their eyes were not being punished because their fingernails were in good condition.

If you ask me, I would say that virtue is much more valuable than wealth just as eyes are much more valuable than fingernails.

[*Source:* Stobaeus, I.3,50]

14. A sense of shame keeps us in the right track

Let us consider the morose philosophers [*as Stoic philosophers were portrayed by Epicurus*] who say that pleasure is itself not in agreement with nature but a mere byeproduct of what is in agreement with nature, such as justice, self-control, and freedom.

Epicurus challenges: Why then, does the mind delight in and find peace in the lesser goods of the body? Why doesn't it take pleasure in its own superior goods?

[*To which I respond*] Well, nature has given us the sense of shame. I often blush when I catch myself doing something shameful. It is this sense of shame that will not allow me to lay down pleasure as the good, and pleasure as the end of life.

[*Source:* Stobaeus, III.6,57]

15. People delight in finding excuses for their faults

The women in Rome carry around Plato's Republic because it calls for a community of women. They attend only to the words of the author, and not to what he meant. He does not say that one man and one woman should marry and live together, hoping to create a community of wives based on that. He wants to abolish that kind of marriage and introduce a different kind to replace it.

People, in general, delight in finding excuses for their faults. Yet philosophy says we should not even stretch out a finger without good reason.

[*Source*: Stobaeus, III.6,58]

16. Keep reminding yourself of the basic principles

We should know that it is not easy for us to form a [right] judgement, unless we say and hear the same principles every day, and, at the same time, apply them all to our lives.

[*Source:* Stobaeus, III.29,84]

17. Appreciate what you have in front of you

We are invited to a dinner party. We take what is given to us. If a guest orders the host to give fish or cakes instead, he would be thought of as rude. Yet, in real life, we ask of God what he does not give us. We do this even though he has given us plenty.

[*Source:* Stobaeus, III.4,91]

18. Your value comes from your virtue, not from externals

"These are charming people," Epictetus said "who take great pride in things not under their control."

One person says, 'I am a better person than you, because I have more properties than you, while you are practically starving,'; another person says, 'I'm an important official,' or 'I'm a governor;' yet another person says 'I have thick curly hair.'

One horse does not say to another 'I'm better than you because I have lots of hay and barley; I have gold bridles and an embroidered saddle," but "I'm better because I am faster than you. Every animal is better or worse depending on its virtue or defect.

Are human beings the only ones lacking in virtue of our own? Must we, instead, take into account our hair, clothes, and ancestry?

[*Source:* Stobaeus, III.4,92]

---

19. Appreciate what you have in front of you

People who are sick are annoyed with a doctor who doesn't give them advice, because they think the doctor has given up on them. Shouldn't we feel the same about a philosopher who stops telling us anything of use and conclude that he has given up hope of our becoming rational?

[*Source:* Stobaeus, III.4,93]

---

20. Develop a strong mind to withstand emotions

Those who are in good physical condition are able to tolerate heat and cold. Likewise, those whose are good mental condition can handle anger and grief, excessive joy, and other emotions.

[Source: Stobaeus, III.4,94]

---

21. Accept anything that comes your way

It is right to praise Agrippinus for this reason: Although he was a man of highest character, he never praised himself; if someone else praised him, he only became embarrassed. His character was such that, when he faced any hardship he would praise it. If he had a fever, in praise of fever; if he faced disgrace, in favour of disgrace; if he was exiled, in praise of exile. And once, when he was about to dine, a messenger interrupted him with the news that Nero sentenced him to exile. 'Well, then, he said, 'we will dine in Aricia.' [*Aricia was a town outside Rome.*]

[Source: Stobaeus, III.7,16]

---

22. Don't condemn wrong-doers

When Agrippinus was governor, he would try to convince those whom he sentenced that it was for their own good they are sentenced. 'I don't condemn them as their enemy, or as a robber, but as their protector and guardian, like a doctor who comforts a man being operated on so he can submit himself to the operation.

[Source: Stobaeus, IV.7,44]

23. Care for your body, but be ready to release it

Nature is wonderful and 'loves her creatures,' as Xenophon says. Consider the body – the most unpleasant and dirtiest thing – we take care of it all the same. If we had to look after our neighbour's body, even for just five days, we could not bear it. Imagine what it would be like to get up in the morning, brush someone else's teeth and then, after their attending the call of nature, wash their private parts. It is truly amazing that we can love something that demands so much of our services on a daily basis. [Pointing to his belly] 'I stuff this bag and empty it again. What is more troublesome?' But I must serve God. For that reason, I stay and put up with feeding and housing this miserable body. When I was younger, it asked of me something else and yet I put up with it. So why can't you tolerate giving back your body when nature, which gave you the body, asks for it back?

"But I love it."

"But wasn't it nature, as I just said, that made you love it? It is the same nature that also says now, 'let go of your body. Have no trouble with it anymore.'"

[*Source:* Stobaeus, IV.53,29]

24. People neither want to live, nor die

Whenever someone dies young, they blame the gods because they died before their proper time. But when they fail to die when old, they also blame the gods, because at the time when he should be resting, he has trouble. Yet, when it is time to die, he wishes to live and sends for his doctor and begs him to spare no effort or zeal. "People are strange," Epictetus said, "they neither want to live nor die."

[*Source: Stobaeus*, IV.53,30]

25. Avoid aggressive behaviour

When you set about attacking someone with violence and aggression, remind yourself that you are not a savage animal. This way, you will never do anything brutal and, in the end, you will have nothing to regret or to explain.

[*Source:* Stobaeus, III.20,67]

26. You are a soul in a mortal body

You are a little soul carrying around a corpse, as Epictetus used to say.

[*Source:* Marcus Aurelius, *Meditations* IV.41]

27. Handle your desires and aversions with care

Epictetus said that we must discover an art of managing assent. Where choices are concerned, we must pay careful and close attention, and exercise them with reservation and merit to serve the society. We must stay away from desire altogether and not seek to avoid anything that is not under our control.

[*Source:* Marcus Aurelius, *Meditations* XI.37]

28. Your sanity is at stake

"It is no ordinary matter that is stake here," Epictetus said, "but it is a question of either madness or sanity."

[*Source:* Marcus Aurelius, *Meditations* XI.38]

28a. You will not fight if you are rational and sound

Socrates would say, "What do you want? To have the souls of rational or irrational animals?"

"Rational animals."

"What kind of rational animals? Sound or vicious?"

"Sound."

"Why don't you work at it, then?"

"Because we have them already."

"Then why are you still fighting and quarrelling?"

[*Source:* Marcus Aurelius, *Meditations* II.39]

28b. Nothing that happens to you is a misfortune

Don't say,

"Poor me. This happened to me."

Say instead,

"Lucky me. This happened to me. Although this has happened to me, I am still happy. I am not crushed by the present nor afraid of the future."

This could have happened to anyone. Yet not everyone would have remained untroubled by it.

Why treat the former as misfortune and not the latter as good fortune? Do you call anything a person's misfortune that's not a perversion of human nature? Don't you think a perversion of human nature runs against nature's will? What then? You already know the nature of human will. So, this misfortune that happened to you does not stop you in any way in being just, generous, self-controlled, reasonable, careful, free from deceit, courteous, free, etc., all of which together make human nature complete, does it?

Remember from now on, whenever something begins to trouble you, make use this principle:

This is no misfortune. To endure it and prevail is good fortune.

[*Source:* Marcus Aurelius, *Meditations* IV.49,2-6]

SAYINGS OF EPICTETUS
OF DOUBTFUL AUTHENTICITY

Fragments that are of doubtful authenticity are presented here. They are attributed to Epictetus. Even though their authenticity is dubious, we cannot entirely dismiss them as inauthentic. They are presented below.

29. Avoid saying things that don't make sense

Under all conditions, take care of nothing as much as safety. It is safer to be silent than to speak. Avoid saying things that make no sense and are full of criticism.

[*Source:* Stobaeus, III.35,10. Stobaeus attributes this quote to *Enchiridion*. But *Enchiridion* contains no such passage. It is doubtful if Epictetus even said this.]

30. Don't depend on a single hope

We should neither fasten our ship to one small anchor, nor our life to a single hope.

[*Source:* Stobaeus, IV.46,22]

31. Don't depend on a single hope

We should measure the length of our stride, and the extent of our hope, by what is possible.

[*Source:* Stobaeus, IV.46,23]

32. Death is better than a bad life

It is much more necessary to cure the soul than the body. Death is better than a bad life.

[*Source:* Stobaeus, IV.53,27.
This quote has also been attributed to many others.]

33. Rare pleasure and more delightful

Pleasure that comes more rarely gives the greatest delight.

[*Source*: Stobaeus, III.6,59; Democritus, *Fragments* 232.]

34. Be moderate

Once you exceed moderation, the most delightful things may become the least delightful.

[*Source*: Stobaeus, III.6,60; Democritus, *Fragments* 233.]

35. To be free, master yourself

No man is free who is not a master of himself.

[*Source:* Florilegium. Cod. Paris 1168 (501E);
Stobaeus ascribes this to Pythagoras.]

36. Truth is eternal

The truth is something immortal and eternal. It does not present us with a beauty that fades with time, nor free speech which can be taken away by justice, but it presents us with what is just and lawful, different from what is unlawful and challenging it.

[*Source*: Antonius 1.21. According to W.A. Oldfather, this style is too alien to Epictetus and so of doubtful authenticity.]

PART 3

The Golden Sayings
of Epictetus

1. Remember God's gift us and be thankful

Are these the only signs that providence gave us? Hardly! In fact, there are no words adequate to do justice to them or praise them. If we had any sense, there is nothing better we could do with our time than praise God and appreciate his good works, publicly and privately and remember the benefits he bestows upon us. We should praise him even when we are busy digging, ploughing, or eating.

"God is great – he has given us these instruments to work on the earth."

"God is great – he has given us hands, a mouth, and a stomach."

"God is great – he has given us the ability to grow unconsciously and breath in our sleep."

This is what we ought to sing on every occasion, celebrating the ability he has given us to understand and use his works systematically. This is the greatest and the holiest of hymns.

But most of you have become blind. Someone has to fill this role and praise God on your behalf. What else can a lame old man like me do except sing God's praises? If I were a nightingale or a swan, I would sing like either of them was born to sing. But I am a rational being, so my song is a hymn. This is my job and I will do it. I will continue to sing as long as I am permitted. I invite you to join me.

[*Source*: *Discourses* I.16, 15-19]

---

2. Don't be distracted by incidental attractions

What do people usually do? They behave like a traveller returning home who comes across an inn, finds it comfortable and stays there. Have you forgotten your purpose? You were not traveling to this, but through this.

"But this is a fine inn."

"Sure. There are many other fine inns and many pleasant pastures. They are just way stations. Your business is to return to your country, to relieve the anxieties of your family, and be a citizen; to get married, raise children, and be employed."

You did not come into this world to pick the most charming place to live but to live in the country of your birth or in a country of which you are a citizen.

[*Source*: *Discourses* II.23, 36-39]

3. Enjoy the festival of life

Try to enjoy the festival of life with others.

[*Source*: *Discourses* IV.4, 26]

4. Obey God and His rules

But I have one whom I must please, whom I must submit to, whom I must obey – that is God and, after that, myself. He has entrusted me to myself and made my choice subject to myself alone, and gave me rules for the right use of it.

[*Source*: *Discourses* IV.12, 11-12]

5. A philosopher moves the audience and does not seek praise

Rufus used to say "If you find leisure time to praise me, my speech was a failure." He would speak in such a way to make everyone who heard him supposed that someone had informed on him. Such was his understanding of how people behave that he vividly placed each man's private fault in front of him.

[Source: *Discourses* III.23, 29]

6. Judging your impressions correctly will set you free

Why are the other faculties [other than reason] not placed under our power? We would have been given power over other faculties too, but we are on Earth and bound to a physical body and material things. Therefore we cannot avoid being limited by external things. Even our bodies are not truly our own, but just cleverly constructed to seem that way. Given these limitations, it is as if God, because he could not give us control over our body, making it free of restraint, has given us a portion of himself.

Reason gives us the ability to act or not act and to desire something or move toward or away from it by properly judging our perceptions or impressions. If we pay attention to just this one thing, we will never be hindered and we will never complain, flatter, or find fault. Does this seem like a small gift to you? Of course not!

[*Source*: *Discourses* I,1.7-10]

7. Don't worry about what others say

Haven't you heard what [the philosopher] Antisthenes said: "It's a king's lot, Cyrus, to do well, and be spoken ill of."

[*Source*: *Discourses* IV.6, 20]

8. Decide for yourself what you'll sell yourself for

Did you say it is beneath you? It is for you to decide, not for me. It is you who know yourself, the value you place on yourself, and the price at which you would sell yourself. Different people sell themselves at different prices.

Florus [the financial officer of Judea under Emperor Nero] was debating whether to enter and contribute to the emperor Nero's festival. Agrippinus told him:

"If you are considering it, go and perform."

"Why don't you go to the shows yourself?"

"Because, I wouldn't even consider it."

Once you start placing a value on external things, you come close to a person who has lost all sense of their character. If you ask me, "Is death preferred or life?" I say, "Life." If you ask, "Pain or pleasure?" I say, "Pleasure."

"But if I don't take a part, I could be killed."

"Then go and take a part. But I will not take a part."

"Why?"

"Because you consider yourself as just another thread in a garment. So, you should give thought to acting like all the others. But I consider myself that small shiny purple band in that garment that gives beauty and lustre to others. Don't tell me to be just another thread in the garment. If I did that, then how can I be the purple band? "

[*Source*: *Discourses* I.2, 11-18]

9. We are both animalistic and rational

If you truly believed that we are children of God, as you should, you would not think of yourselves as despicable or inferior in any way. If a king were to adopt you, there would be no end to your conceit. How come you are not proud knowing that you are child of God? In fact, you are not happy at all about this. Why?

Because, from birth, two elements coexist within us: a body that is common to all animals, and a rational mind and intelligence that we share only with God. Unfortunately, we are quick to identify ourselves with animals, even though it is miserable and mortal. Only very few of us identify ourselves with God, even though it is divine and blessed. Everyone will necessarily deal with things according to their beliefs. So those that think that they are born for fidelity and respect, and are confident in their correct use of impressions, will not entertain any mean or ignoble thoughts about themselves. But the majority does the opposite and says, "Who am I but a poor, miserable piece of flesh?" Yes, the flesh is miserable. But you are better than the flesh. Why turn away from this fact and hang on to something that is mortal?

[Source: Discourses I.3, 1-6]

---

10. You are burdened with a body

You are a poor soul burdened with a lifeless body.

[Source: Fragment; M. Antonius IV.41, Schweigh clxxvi]

---

11. You can only lose what you have

Something like this happened to me the other day. I had an iron lamp which I keep by my household shrine. I heard a noise from the window, ran down, and found it stolen. I reasoned that the thief had an irresistible impulse to steal it. I said to myself, "Tomorrow get a cheaper, earthenware lamp. You can only lose what you have."

[Source: Discourses I.18, 5]

12. Everything has a price

That's how I came to lose my lamp – the thief was better at keeping awake than I. But he had a price to pay for the lamp: for its sake, he became a thief, lost his ability to be trusted, and became a brute.

[Source: Discourses I.29, 21]

13. We should end as rational being, even if we begin as animals

But we are brought into this world to witness the work of the creator. Not just to witness but to appreciate it as well. So, it is shameful for a human being to begin and end where irrational animals do. We should begin where they do, but only end in contemplation and understanding, and adopt a way of life in harmony with nature. So, take care not to die without being a witness to these things.

[Source: Discourses I.6, 19-22]

14. Quit complaining and realize your strengths

You travel long distances to see works of art and put many things on your bucket list. You think it would be unfortunate to die without seeing what is on your list. But to see the work of the creator, you don't need to travel anywhere. It's where you are standing right now. Don't you ever want look at it, understand who you are, why you were born, and why you received the gift of sight?

You may say unpleasant and difficult things happen in life. Quite so. Suppose you get to a beautiful place. Then what? Won't you get hot? Won't you find it crowded? Won't you get soaked when it rains? Won't it be noisy? Won't you find other irritations? Knowing all this, you still go there because you think the beauty of the place is worth it.

Have you not received the inner strength to cope with any difficulty that may arise? Have you not been given strength, courage, and patience? Why then should you worry about what happens, when you are armed with these virtues and have the power to endure? What could possibly constrain, compel, or even annoy you? You don't see all this. Instead you moan, groan, shed tears, and complain.

[*Source*: *Discourses* I.6, 23-29]

15. Be a citizen of the universe

If what philosophers say about our kinship with God is true, then it is only logical we are citizens of the universe, not of any particular country. When asked where he was from, Socrates never replied that he was from Athens or Corinth, but always, "I am a citizen of the universe."

[*Source*: *Discourses* I.9.1]

16. Be free of fear and grief

Those who know how the whole universe is administered know the first all-inclusive government is that of God and us. It is the source of all beings, going back generations upon generations, covering every creature ever born and bred on this earth. This is particularly true of rational beings since they alone are entitled by nature to be associated with God through reason.

Why not identify ourselves as citizens of the universe and children of God? Why should we fear any human condition? You may think if you are related to a king, or to some other powerful person, you can live safely and without fear. But you are related to God. Shouldn't you be free of grief and fear?

[Source: Discourses I.9, 4-7]

17. Don't think small

I'm an old man and I shouldn't be trying to persuade you not to think so small.

On the other hand, some young people among you may know your relationship to God; know that you are chained by your body, by your possessions, and other needs of your daily life. You may try to get rid of these things. But I would discourage you from doing so. It is your teacher's job to guide you. You should go to your teacher and say, "We no longer want to be tied to our body, possessions, and other things that bind us; we don't want to be associated with uncongenial people. All such things are indifferent to us. Here we have thieves, robbers, law courts, and people who think they have some power over us because of our body and possessions. Allow us to show them that they have power over no one."

[Source: Discourses I.9, 10-15]

18. Be content to be where you are

If I were your teacher, I would say, "Friends, wait for God's signal for your release from service. Then go. For now, be content to be in the place he stationed you. Your stay here is brief and it is easy enough to endure for people with your level of understanding. No tyrant, thief, or court of law can harm someone who places little value on body and possessions. So, stay here, don't depart without good reason."

[*Source*: *Discourses* I.9, 16.17]

19. Be a citizen of the universe

In reality, this is not how teachers and young students behave. Instead, as soon as you eat your meal today, you sit and worry about tomorrow's meal. I say to you, "If you get it, you will have it. If not, you will depart this life. The door is open. Why cry and complain? Why flatter or envy others? Why admire those with possessions, especially when they are powerful and quick to anger? What can they do to us? Or for us? Things they control are of no interest to us. What we care about, they cannot control. When we think this way, no one is our master. We cannot be made to act against our will."

[*Source*: *Discourses* I.9, 18-22]

20. You have all the resources you need

Now you know all this, appreciate all the resources you have. When you are done, say, "Let any difficulty come my way. I have the resources and a constitution given to me by my creator to deal with whatever happens."

But no, there you sit, trembling with fear about what might happen in the future and upset about things that are happening now. You blame God. How does such weakness help? Yet God has given you the strength to tolerate trouble without being humiliated. He has also provided you a means to be free of constraint, hindrance, or compulsion, without having to fall apart. You have all these powers given to you which God himself cannot take away. Yet you don't use them. You don't even realize what powers you have and where they came from. You refuse to acknowledge your creator and his gifs. Some of you don't even acknowledge his existence.

I am ready to show you that you have resources, strength of character, and resilience. I challenge you to show me what grounds you have to be complaining and reproachful.

[*Source*: *Discourses* I.6, 37-43]

21. Know your affinity to God

How did Socrates feel about these things? Just like someone who knows the affinity between him and God.

[*Source*: *Discourses* I.9, 22]

22. If you want, you are free

If God had made it possible for his own fragment (that is us) to be hindered or compelled by anyone including himself, then he wouldn't be God, looking after us the way he has been.

The diviner says, "That's what I see inscribed in the sacrifice. This is God's signal to you: If you want, you are free. If you want, you will blame no one, you will accuse no one – if you want, everything will happen according to your plan, as well as God's."

[Source: Discourses I.17, 27-28]

23. Avoid rigid thinking

Rigidity can come about in two ways: Either one's intellect is frozen, or one's sense of honour is. Such a person neither agrees to what is true nor leaves the argument altogether. Most of us will go to great lengths to avoid deadening the body; our souls, not so much.

When a person does not see the contradiction in his thinking and is incapable of following an argument, we think he is in a bad way. But when someone sees the contradiction but still does not acknowledge it, when he has no sense of shame, we call it strength of character. In reality, it is even worse.

[Source: Discourses I.5, 3-5]

24. Be diligent in your pursuit

If we pursue self-development as diligently as people after power pursue their schemes, we might get somewhere. I know someone who is older than me and works for the state as an official in charge of the grain supply. When he returned, being out of power for a while, he talked to me about his former life with disdain and said,

"I would give myself exclusively to a life of peace and tranquillity from now on. Not much time left of my life."
"I don't believe you. Your resolve will last only as long as you don't have access to power. The moment that happens, you will forget all this."
"Epictetus, if I ever put one foot in the palace, think of me whatever you like."
How did he act? Even before he entered Rome, he received his letter of appointment. He immediately forgot all he'd said and has not given it a thought ever since. He is piling one encumbrance on another. I should be glad if he passed through this place and talked to me. He made me feel as clever as a prophet compared to him.
Am I saying that he is like an animal unfit for action? Not at all ... and yet how can the business of the state compare to ours? If you look at what they do, you will see. What do they do except vote on a resolution and then huddle together discussing some means of making a living? ... [I, on the other hand, ask you to] learn how the universe works, where we rational beings fit in it, and where good and evil lie."

[*Source*: *Discourses* I.10, 1-10]

25. Misfortune is not evil

A man, who was once wealthy and eminent, came to see me. He had fallen to bad times, lost everything, and asked me to write a letter to Rome on his behalf. I wrote a submissive letter. He read it and returned to me saying that he needed my help, not my pity, and that he faced no evil.

[*Source*: *Discourses* I.9, 27-28]

26. Know your affinity to God

"What is the true instruction, then?"

"Learn to will that things happen as they do."

"And how do they happen?"

"As God wills."

He willed there be summer and winter, abundance and famine, virtue and vice, and all such opposites for the sake of harmony in the universe.

[*Source*: *Discourses* I.12, 15-16]

27. When you lose something, think what you gained in its place

You should always think this when you lose any external thing: What did you get in return? If it was of greater value, don't you say you lost anything.

[*Source*: *Discourses* IV.3, 1]

28. God cares for us

There are different views of God:

- God doesn't exist at all.
- God exists, but doesn't care about anything.
- God exists and cares, but only about heavenly matters, not about earthly ones.
- God exists, and cares about what happens on earth, but not about individuals.
- God exists, and cares about everything, including individual welfare.

Socrates accepted the last view, when he said, "Not a move do I make that you do not see."

[*Source*: *Discourses* I.12, 1-3]

---

29. Freedom is glorious

An intelligent person examines all these arguments and submits his mind to the ruler of the universe, just like good citizens submit to the laws of the state.

If you want to learn, you should come with the following questions:

• How can I follow God in everything?
• How can I live in happiness under divine governance?
• How can I become free?

You are free if everything that happens to you happens according to your choice and not against it.

"Is freedom madness, then?"

"Freedom and madness are incompatible with each other."

"But I wish that anything that I desire happens as I wish."

"You are crazy. You have lost your senses. Don't you know that freedom is a good and valuable thing? To wish that unconsidered things happen at random according to your desire is not valuable, it is shameful."

[*Source*: *Discourses* I.12, 7-12]

---

30. Practice the principles daily

You must know that is not easy for a principle to become your own, unless you maintain it and hear it maintained, and practice it in life.

[*Source*: Fragment, Schweigh lxxii; Shenkl 16]

31. Avoid finding faults and enjoy life

You gripe and protest. When you are alone you say you are lonely. When you are with people, you find fault with them, even if they are your parents, children, spouse, and neighbours. What you should do instead is this: When you are alone call it peace and freedom; when you are in company, instead of calling it a crowd and being annoyed, call it a festival. Learn to enjoy it.

[*Source*: *Discourses* I.12, 20-21]

32. The penalty for not accepting reality is to be the way you are now

What is the penalty for not accepting the things the way they are? To be just the way you are: miserable when alone and unhappy when with others. If you are unhappy with your parents, be a bad son and grumble. If you are unhappy with your children, be a bad father. There is no need to throw you in prison, you are already in one. Whatever place you are in, if you are there against your will, you are in prison. But even if you are in prison, if it is by your will, then you are free. This is the reason Socrates was not imprisoned, because he was there willingly.

[*Source*: *Discourses* I.12, 22-23]

33. Your rationality is on par with God's

Don't you realize your insignificance in the larger scheme of things? That is about the body. But, as far as reason is concerned, you are on par with God. The greatness of reason is not measured by size but by the quality of its judgments. So, would you rather not be equal to God?

[*Source*: *Discourses* I.12, 26-27]

34. Be restrained and controlled

Someone asked Epictetus: "How one can eat in a way pleasing to God?"

"If you ate with restraint and self-control, would that not be pleasing to God? You ask the waiter to bring hot water. She brings lukewarm water or even totally ignores you. If you don't get angry then, would it not be pleasing to God?"

"How can I tolerate such people?"

"The same way you would tolerate your brother, who has the same God for a father. Why do you have to put yourself above him?"

If you are placed in a position above others, are you going to behave like a tyrant? Won't you remember who you are and who you are placed above? They are your kin, siblings by nature, and descendants of the same God. You pay for their services, you say? You are concerned with the laws of the earth, laws of the dead, not laws of God.

[*Source*: *Discourses* I.13]

35. Appreciate what is in front of you

We are invited to a dinner party. We take what is given to us. If a guest orders the host to give fish or cakes instead, he would be thought of as rude. Yet, in real life, we ask of God what he does not give us. We do this even though e has given us plenty.

[Source: Fragments (Stobaeus) Schwiegh xv; Shenckl 17]

36. God watches over us

Someone wanted to know how one can be sure that God watches over each of our actions. Epictetus asked:

"Do you not see unity in everything?"

"I do."

"Don't you think that things on earth feel the influence of heaven?"

"Yes."

How else could things happen with such precise regularity, if God weren't issuing orders? He orders plants to bloom and they bloom. He tells them to bear fruit and they do so. When he tells them to ripen, they ripen. Again, when he tells them to drop their fruit, shed their leaves, lie dormant in winter, they obey. How else to explain the waxing and waning of the moon, coming and going of the sun, and changes and fluctuations on earth? If plants and our bodies are so influenced, wouldn't it be more true of our minds? If our minds are so intimately connected with God and a part of his being, would he not be aware of their every motion?

[Source: Discourses I.14-16]

37. God has given you a guardian

"But I cannot understand all these things at once."

"Did anyone say that you have the capacities that are equal to God's? No!"

Yet he has provided every one of us with a personal guardian deity to stay with us and look after us. This guardian never sleeps and cannot be distracted. Is there a better or more vigilant guardian God could have given us? Whenever you shut your door and turn off the lights, don't say to yourself that you are alone. You are not. God is inside and so is your personal deity. They don't need light to watch over you.

You need to swear allegiance to this God, as soldiers do to the king. If they want to be paid, they must put the king first. You have chosen to receive favours and blessings for free. Why won't you swear a similar allegiance to God? If you have already done so, why won't you abide by it?

"What must you swear?"

"You swear that you will not disobey, accuse, or find fault with God's gifts and that you will not shrink from things that are inevitable."

"Are these oaths similar?"

"Not at all. The soldiers swear to honour just the king; but we swear to honour, above all, our true selves."

[*Source*: *Discourses* I.14, 12-17]

38. Others' anger has nothing to do with you

"Then, how do I stop my brother being angry with me?"

"Bring him to me and I will tell him. I have nothing to say to you about his anger."

[*Source*: *Discourses* I.15.5]

39. Nothing happens instantaneously

"Tell me this then. How can I stay true to nature, even when he refuses to reconcile with me?"

"Nothing important happens in an instant. Even grapes and figs take time to ripen. If you say you want a fig right now, I will ask you to be patient. First let the tree blossom and bear fruit. And then, let the fruit ripen. If the fig tree is not brought to maturity instantly or in an hour, how do you expect the fruit of a human mind to come to fruition in such a short time, and so easily? I tell you, don't expect any such thing."

[*Source*: *Discourses* I.15, 6-8]

40. Externals distort our judgments

Epaphroditus [Epictetus' owner when he was a slave] once sold a slave because he was useless. The slave, who was a shoemaker, was bought by a member of Caesar's household. So, he became a shoemaker to the emperor. If only you had seen the way Epaphroditus honoured him!

"How is my friend Felicio today?"

If someone asked us "Where is your master?" he was told, "He is in conference with Felicio."

Hadn't he sold him off because he was useless? How did he become so wise suddenly? Well, that's what happens when we value what is not under our control.

[*Source*: *Discourses* I.19, 19-23]

41. What you avoid for yourself, do not do to others

What you want to avoid facing yourself, do not try impose on others. You avoid slavery? Beware of enslaving others. If you can bear doing that, one would think you had been a slave once yourself. Vice has nothing common with virtue; neither has freedom anything to do with slavery.

[*Source*: *Fragments*. Schwiegh xlii; Shenckl *Gen. Epict. Stob.* 36]

42. We are not grateful for the right things

Someone is promoted. All who meet him congratulate him. They kiss his eyes and cheeks, even hands. At home, lights are lit in his honour. He climbs up the Capitol and offers a sacrifice of thanks. I ask you, who has ever offered thanks for the right desires or for impulses in agreement with nature? It seems that we only thank God for what we believe to be the good things in life.

[*Source*: *Discourses* I.19, 24-25]

43. Don't seek worthless honours

[Epictetus said] A man asked me today about accepting an important public office, the priesthood of Augustus. I told him not to accept.

"You will incur a lot of expense for little return."

"But the clerk will add my name to a public contract."

"OK, you attend the signing ceremonies now. What happens when you die?"

"My name will survive me."

"Carve it in stone, and it will survive equally well. Outside this city, no one will remember this."

"But I get to wear a crown of gold."

"If your heart is set on a crown, make one out of roses. You will look prettier in that."

[*Source*: *Discourses* I.19, 26-29]

44. Don't complain while playing

So, remember that the door is open. Don't be more cowardly than children who say, when they are tired of the game, "I will play no more."

When you feel weary of the game, say "I will play no more" and depart. If you stay, quit complaining.

[*Source*: *Discourses* I.24.20]

45. If it is unbearable, quit; else stay

Is there a smoke in the house? If it is not suffocating, stay. If it is, get out. Always remember: the door is open.

"Don't live in Nicopolis."

"I won't live there."

"Don't live in Athens."

"Okay, I won't live in Athens either."

"Live on Gyara."

But, for me, living on Gyara is like living in a smoky house. So, I go to the one place no one can stop me from going. A place where everyone is welcome. When I remove all my clothing including my skin, then no one can hold me any longer. Thus, Demetrius challenged Nero: "You threaten me with death, but nature threatens you with it."

[Source: Discourses I. 25, 18-22]

46. Don't tackle it, if you cannot handle it

So, if one wants to be a philosopher, one should first become aware of one's governing principle. When a person knows it is in a weak state, he will refrain from tackling difficult matters. The way it is now though, some people who cannot work though a leaflet will try to devour a whole treatise. The result? They get sick or suffer indigestion. Worse things follow. They should first find out what they are capable of.

[Source: Discourses I. 26, 15-16]

47. Examine yourself

In matters of theory, it is easy to refute someone who is ignorant. But, in the affairs of life, no one offers himself to be examined. We resent being examined as well. Yet Socrates used to say that the unexamined life is not worth living.

[Source: Discourses I. 26, 17-18]

48. Your daily practice is your preparation for life's trials

This is why when someone asked Socrates to prepare for the trial, he said

"Don't you think I have been preparing for this my entire life?"

"Preparing for it how?"

"I have minded my own business, never did anything wrong, either in public or in private."

[*Source*: *Discourses* II.2, 8-9]

49. Speak well of others

Do you want people to speak well of you? Speak well of them. When you have learned to speak well of them, try doing something good for them. Then you will benefit from their speaking well of you.

[*Source*: *Fragments*. (Stoaebus: Schwiegh vii]

50. As long as you are playing, don't complain

When you come face to face with a prominent person, remember that there is someone else looking from above. You have to please him first. He asks:

"When you were in school, how were you taught to look upon exile, imprisonment, restraint, death, and disgrace?"

"I was taught they are indifferents."

"What do you say now? Have they changed in any way?"

"No."

"Have you changed?"

"No"

"Tell me what 'indifferents' are."

"Whatever we cannot control."

"The bottom line?"

"They are nothing to me."

"Tell me what good things are."

"Making the right choice and using impressions correctly."

"What is the goal of life?"

"To follow you."

[*Source*: *Discourses* I. 30, 1-4]

51. The body may suffer, but the soul is free

"Are you saying then that it was all right for Socrates to have suffered at the hands of Athenians?"

"Not Socrates, idiot. Say it as it really is. The poor body of Socrates was seized, dragged, and thrown into prison by stronger men. Someone gave his poor body hemlock and it died."

Do you think all this is so unjust that you should blame God? Didn't Socrates have other resources to offset all this? What was the essence of the good for him? Do you want us to listen to you or to him when he said, "Anytus and Meleuts can kill me, but they cannot harm me. If it pleases the gods, so be it."

[*Source*: *Discourses* I. 16-18]

52. Recognize God's signs

No, young man, by the gods let it not be your fate. Once you have heard these words, go home and tell yourself: "It wasn't Epictetus who told me all this. How could he have come up with this? It must be some benevolent god, speaking through him. It would have never entered his mind to say such things, because he is not in the habit of speaking to anyone. Well, let's obey God then and not incur his anger." If a raven gives you a sign through croaking, it isn't the raven but God through him. If God gives a sign through a human voice, will you pretend that it is simply a human being who is saying this to you and fail to recognize the divine voice? Will you not recognize that he gives signs to some people one way, and to other people, another way? And, when it comes to the highest and most important matters, he gives the sign through his noblest messenger? What else does the poet mean when he says: ... since we ourselves warned him, by sending keen-sighted Hermes, the slayer of Argus, neither to murder the man, nor make love to his wife.

[Translation by CG/RH]
[Source: Discourses III.1, 36-38]

53. Speaking your mind has consequences

Consider what my friend Heraclitus did in a trivial lawsuit about a piece of land in Rhodes. After proving his case, he went on to comment, "I don't care what your decision is going to be. I am not on trial, but *you* are." Thus, he lost his case.

[Source: Discourses II.2, 17]

54. Death and pain are not frightening; but the fear on death and pain is

We act like deer that, frightened by feathers, seek safety in hunter's nets. They meet their untimely death by confusing caution with confidence. ... Death and pain are not frightening, but the fear of death and pain are. That's why we praise the person who said, "Death is no ill, but dying like a coward is."

[*Source*: Discourses II.1, 8 and 13]

---

55. Consider the bigger picture

Why do we say, then, some externals are natural, while others are not?

It depends on whether we consider them together or separately. For example, if taken by itself, it is natural for my foot to be clean. But if I consider it as a part of my body, then it is proper for my foot to walk through mud and thorns and step on needles. It may even have to be amputated for the sake of the whole body. It cannot be considered a foot otherwise.

We have to reason that some such distinction applies to us as well. What are you? A human being. If you think of yourself as a separate unit, then it is natural to live to old age, be wealthy and healthy. But when you think of yourself as a part of humanity, then it is natural for you to get sick, face unsafe situations, struggle to make ends meet and even die before your time. Why are you then upset? Don't you realize that just as a foot is no longer a foot when detached from the body, you are not a human being when you are detached from humanity? What is a human being? Part of a state. First, the state which is made up of god and humans. Second, the state where one happens to live, which is a small copy of the universal state.

… We are given such a body as ours, in such a universe as ours, and in such a community as ours. Therefore, what happens to us is unavoidable. It is for you to step forward and deal with these things as best as you can.

Thus, if you are declared guilty, you can tell the judge 'I wish you well. I have done my part. It is for you to decide if you have done yours.' After all, don't forget, the judge runs a risk too.

[*Source: Discourses* II.5, 24-29]

56. Experience and expertise lead to correct judgment

When someone asked Diogenes for a letter of recommendation, he gave him an excellent answer.

"At first glance he will know you are a man. He will also know whether you are good or bad, if he has the ability to distinguish the two. But if he doesn't, he will not discover it, even if I write a thousand letters."

It is like a coin asking for a recommendation for person to declare it authentic. If the person in question is an assayer, the coin would speak for itself.

[*Source: Discourses* II.3, 1-2]

57. Don't have any preference for what you would like to happen

A traveller who reaches a fork on the road, not knowing which road to take doesn't have any preference as to which road she takes, as long as it is the one that will take her to where she wants to go. We should also use God as a guide in the same way, like we use our eyes. We don't ask our eyes to accept only particular impressions, but all that eyes can show us.

Instead, we approach fortune-tellers as if they were gods, imploring them to tell us good news.

You want what is best for you. Now, what is best for you other than what God wishes? Why do you then do everything possible to corrupt your judge, to mislead your counsellor?

[*Source*: *Discourses* II.7, 10-14]

58. Don't have any preference for what you would like to happen

God is helpful. What is good is also helpful. It seems then that where there is the true nature of God, there is also is the true nature of good.

"What, then, is the true nature of God. Is it flesh?"

"Certainly not!"

"Land? Status?"

"Not at all."

The nature of God is in knowledge and right reason. Only here should you look for the true nature of good. You won't find it in plants or animals.

[*Source*: *Discourses* II.8, 1-3]

59. Humans are the principal works for God

"Because the nature of good is absent from both plants and animals, should you not look for it in that quality that distinguishes humans from all other things?"

"Aren't plants and animals works of God?"

"They are. But they are not of primary importance and are not parts of God."

But you are a principal work of God, a fragment of him. You have a part of Him in you. Why are you then ignorant of your noble birth? Why don't you remember your origin? Why don't you remember, when you eat, who you are and whom you are feeding? When you have sex, who is it that's doing it? Whenever you converse, exercise, or socialize, don't you know that it is with God you do these things?

You carry God around you and you don't know it, poor fool! I am not talking about some external god made of silver of gold. The God you carry around with you is a living one and yet you are so blind to the fact that you defile Him with your impure thoughts and offensive behaviour. You wouldn't repeat such behaviour even when a god's statue is nearby. When God himself is there within you, and sees and hears everything you do and say, are you not ashamed to think and act the way you do? You are not aware of your own nature and are an object of God's anger.

[*Source*: *Discourses* II.8, 9-14]

60. God want you take care of yourself

What are we anxious about when we send out a young man into the real world after he graduates from school? That he may make mistakes, eat poorly, have affairs, humiliate himself, and dress in poor clothes or dress to impress? Why? Because he is ignorant of that God is within him. He fails to realize who goes with him and says, "I wish you were here with me." Is it not so that God is with him wherever he goes?

Having Him with you, why look for someone else? Would they tell you any different?

If you were a sculpture made by [the famous sculptor] Phidias, then you would have remembered who you are and who it is that made you. If you had any intelligence, you would try to avoid doing anything unworthy of your creator or of you, such as making yourself a spectacle in front of others. God made you. Are you then unconcerned about the spectacle you make of yourself? How can you even compare the creations of a sculptor with creations of God?

What other work of art comes with all the powers that the artist displayed while making it? Is it anything more than marble, bronze, gold, or ivory? Phidias' statue of Athena, once finished with its arms raised to support Victory, remains that way forever. The works of God, on the other hand, are living, breathing beings. They can deal with impressions and test them. When you are the work of such an artist, will you discredit him – especially when he not only created you but has given you complete control over yourself? You not only forget that, but dishonour the trust he placed in you.

If God had asked you to care for some orphans, would you have ignored them? God has asked you to care for yourself, saying, "I don't have anyone more dependable than you. Preserve this person for me along with the qualities nature has given him: modesty, faithfulness, dignity, patience, calmness, and poise." Will you not keep him so? ...

I will show you that I am the kind of person who is faithful, honourable, noble, and poised.

"Do you mean to say that you are immune from illness, death, age, and disease?"

"No, but I would die and bear disease God-like. This much is in my power. This I can do."

[*Source*: *Discourses* II.8, 15-23, 27-28]

61. No labour is good if it doesn't produce courage and strength

According to Diogenes, no labour is good if it does not aim at producing courage and strength of soul rather than of body.

[*Source*: Fragment (Stobaeus. Schweigh lvii]

62. Don't ridicule those who've lost their way

If a guide finds someone who has lost his way, she would not ridicule or abuse him or walk away from him, but show him the right path. So, it is your job to show the other person the right path and you will see that he follows it. But as long as you have not done this, don't make fun of him but recognize that you have not done your part.

[*Source*: *Discourses* II.12, 3-4]

63. Be careful not to provoke while arguing

Socrates was well-known for remaining unprovoked in an argument and not being abusive even when insulted; he would be patient with the opponent and put an end to the conflict. Would you like to know how good he was at this? Then read Xenophon's *Symposium*. You'll see how many disputes he ended. Even poets praised this quality of his with these words:

"He could cut short a dispute, however great, with his skill."

Engaging in logical dialogs is not a safe business any more, especially in Rome. If you pursue logic, you cannot do it in a corner. You find someone rich and powerful and ask him:

"Sir, do you know who is looking after your horses?"

"I do."

"Is it the first person who came along, whether he knew anything about horses or not?"

"Of course not."

"What about your money? Your clothes?"

"No, I don't hand over these to the first person who comes along."

"Do you have someone who looks after your body?"

"Yes, of course."

"I presume to an expert in exercise and medicine?"

"Yes."

"Are these the things you value most or do you have something even better?"

"What do you mean?"

"The faculty that uses, tests, and thinks about all these things."

"You mean my soul?"

"Exactly. That's what I mean."

"Absolutely. It is by far the best thing I possess. Better than all other things."

"Then tell me how you take care of your soul. Surely someone as wise and respected as you are would not neglect and ruin the most precious thing you have?"

"Certainly not."

"Do you take care of it yourself? If so, did you learn how from someone else or did you discover it yourself?"

At this point, you are entering the danger zone with the other person responding with, "How is this your business? Are you my boss?" If you persist, he may punch you in the face. I am speaking from experience. I used to be keen on such discourses – until I met with such troubles.

[*Source*: *Discourses* II.12, 14-25]

64. Don't claim credit for others' qualities

When a young person was boasting in the Theatre saying, "I'm wise, for have talked with many wise people," Epictetus replied, I have talked with many rich people, yet I am not rich?"

[*Source*: Fragment. Schweigh clxx (v. Asmus p.20)]

65. Model yourself after God

If you want to be a carpenter or a pilot, you need some formal training. It is the same here as well. It is not enough to wish to become wise and good, we need to learn certain things. We must find out what they are. The philosophers tell us that we should first learn that there is a God and that He provides for the Universe. We cannot keep our actions – or even our intentions and thoughts – hidden from Him. Then we must learn about the divine nature. If we want to please the gods, we must obey them and try to resemble them to the best of our ability. If the divine nature is trustworthy, we should be trustworthy; if the divine nature is free, benevolent, and compassionate, we should be free, benevolent, and compassionate as well. We should use God as our model for our thoughts and behaviour.

[*Source*: *Discourses* II.14, 10-13]

66. The missing key to happiness

What if I could show you that you are missing the key to happiness? That you have spent all these days on things that are not right for you? That, to top it all, you don't know what God is, what a human being is and what good and evil are? If I say you are ignorant of these things, you may bear with me. But, if I add that you don't even know who you are, how can you tolerate it? Will you be patient, put up with my questioning and stay with me? Not at all. You'll be offended and leave immediately.

Yet, what harm have I done to you? None. No more than a mirror that shows a plain person for what she looks like. Or a doctor who tells the patient, "Do you think you are well? No, you are sick. Don't eat anything today. Just drink water." No one says, "How rude!" But if I say to anyone, "Your desires are unhealthy, your attempts to avoid things are humiliating, your purposes are confused, your choices are at odds with nature, and your values are random and false," he immediately walk out saying, "Epictetus insulted me."

[*Source*: *Discourses* II.14, 19-22]

67. Reflect on how life works

This is similar to what happens when you attend a fair where cattle are bought and sold. Most people are there to buy and sell cattle. But there a few who come just to see how the fair is organized, who is promoting it and why. The "fair" of the world in which we live is no different. Some people, like cattle, care only for their food. Your possessions, property, large household with servants, and public status are nothing more than cattle fodder.

A few others who attend the fair are capable of reflecting, "What is this world? Who runs it? No one?" No city or a house can function even for a short time without someone taking care of it. And can this design, so vast and so beautiful, run on its own, by mere chance? Therefore, there must be somebody who governs it. But who is he? How does he govern? What are we who were made by him? What purpose are we here to fulfil? Are we connected to Him or not? They think about these things, make time for this, and learn as much as possible about the festival of life before they leave the fair.

The result? They are laughed at by others, just as spectators would be laughed at by traders. And as cattle would laugh at those who are interested in anything other than fodder, if they had any understanding.

[*Source*: *Discourses* II.14, 23-29]

---

68. A fool is inflexible

Now I understand the meaning of the proverb, (which I didn't understand before) "A fool you can neither bend nor break." I hope I never have a clever fool for a friend. "I have decided!" he says. So do crazy people. The more delusional they are, the more medication they need.

[*Source*: *Discourses* II.15, 23-29]

69. Be happy wherever you are

"Will I ever see my native city and the city I grew up in?"

"You poor man. Aren't you happy with where you are? What can you see anywhere that is better than the sun, the moon, the stars, the land, and the sea? If you understand that the God you carry within you governs everything, why would you go looking for marble and fine stones? What will you do when it is time for you leave the sun and moon behind? Will you sit down and cry like a baby?"

What did you do in your school? What did you hear? What did you learn? Why do you call yourself a philosopher when all you did was learn a few elementary things and bit of Chrysippus? You hardly crossed the threshold of philosophy.

[*Source*: *Discourses* II.16, 32-34]

70. Look for happiness where it is, not where it is not

As the saying goes, "Man, do something desperate to achieve freedom and tranquillity. Lift your head up, like someone released from slavery. Dare to face God and say, "Use me as you like from now on. I am yours and of one mind with you. I refuse nothing that you judge to be good. Lead me where you will. Clothe me in any dress. If it is your will, I will hold any position: officer or citizen, rich or poor, stay here or be banished. No matter what, I will defend you before others. I will show the true nature of things, as they really are."

That's not what you do, is it? You sit indoors waiting for your mother to come and feed you. Imagine what would have happened if [the divine hero in Greek mythology] Heracles had simply hung around the house. He would have been [the cowardly king] Eurystheus, not Heracles. Think about the many friends and companions Heracles made, because he travelled the world. None was closer to him than God and so he was believed to be the son of God. In obedience to God, he went around rooting out crime and injustice. You are no Heracles, you cannot root out the crimes and injustice of others. You are not even [the ancient king] Theseus, otherwise you would relieved the evils of Attica.

Then the least you can do is to get your house in order. Instead of getting rid of robbers, get rid of sorrow, fear, lust, envy, and *schadenfreude* (joy at others' misfortunes), greed, petulance, and over-indulgence. But to do this, you need to look up to God and God only and follow His guidance. If you are unwilling to do this you will end up in sighs and tears. You will be forced to serve someone physically stronger than you. You will seek happiness outside yourself, and will never find it. It is because you will be looking for happiness in a place where it is not rather than in a place where it really is.

[*Source: Discourses* II.16, 41-47]

71. If you think you already know, you cannot learn

What is the first order of business when you start learning philosophy? To set aside your self-satisfaction about what you think you know. You are not going to learn anything new, if you think you know it already.

[*Source: Discourses* II.17, 1]

72. Be single-minded in your pursuit

Give me a young student who comes to the school with this single purpose, like an athlete in action: "I don't care about the rest. All I want is to spend my life free of obstruction and distress, hold up my head high no matter what happens, and be a free person, a friend of God, fearing nothing that can happen." If any of you can show me that you are such a person, I would say, "Come in, young man, to claim what is your own. You are a credit to philosophy. Yours are all these possessions, books, and discourses.

Thus, when the student learns and masters the first area of study, comes back to me and says, "I want to be free from fear and emotions. Not just that. As a respectful, philosophical, careful, and attentive person, I would like to know my duty to God, to my parents, siblings, country, and to strangers," I would ask the student to progress to this second area of study.

When the student has mastered the second area of study as well and says, "I have mastered this second area. Now I would like to be secure and unshakable, not just when I am awake but even when I am asleep, drunk, or depressed." My response would be, "You are God. Your goals are praiseworthy!"

[*Source*: *Discourses* II.17, 29-33]

73. Are we our senses?

"The question is at stake," Epictetus said, "is no common one; it is this: Are we in our senses or are we not?"

[Source: Fragment. *(M. Antonius);*
Schweigh clxxviii; Shenckl 28]

74. If you don't want a habit, don't feed it

When you are angry, it is not an isolated bad thing. You have encouraged a habit, adding fuel to the fire. When you yield to lust, don't think of it as a temporary setback. You have fed and strengthened your weakness. You can expect habits to get stronger by actions associated with them. This is how current habits become stronger and newer habits are formed.

Here is how you become mentally weak, according to philosophers. When you become greedy, if you use reason to alert you to the danger, your passion will subside and your mind will be returned to its former balance. But if you don't do anything, the mind will not return to its balanced state, but will be excited by another impression, yielding to passion even more quickly. If you keep yielding to passion, the mind will become insensitive to greed. Eventually, greed will become entrenched.

If you had fever and recovered, you are not in the same state as before, unless you are fully cured. This is true of the unhealthy passions of the mind as well. They leave certain scars and traces behind. Unless you make sure that you are totally cured, the spots that are not fully cured become vulnerable if you have a relapse.

So, if you don't want to be bad-tempered, don't feed the habit. Don't do anything that will strengthen the anger habit. Calm down. Don't be angry today. Or the following day. Count the number of days you can go without getting angry.

"I used to be angry every day. Then every other day. Then every third," and so on. If you manage to spend thirty days without getting angry, give thanks to God.

[*Source*: *Discourses* II.18, 5-12]

75. Be worthy of yourself and of God

How do we resolve it, then? Begin by wanting to please yourself and appear worthy in the presence of God. Desire to become pure in your own eyes and those of God.

[*Source*: *Discourses* II.18, 19]

76. Don't be carried away by impressions

A true trainee is one who trains himself to test any impression that comes his way. Steady yourself, poor thing, don't get carried away by impressions. It is a great battle and it is divine. It is a battle to win your kingdom, freedom, happiness, and serenity. Remember God and ask for his help and protection like sailors do in a storm.

[*Source*: *Discourses* II.18, 27-29]

77. On who walks the walk is hard to find

Who then is a Stoic? We call a statue "Pheidian," if it is made in the style of Pheidias. So, show me someone who shapes himself according his beliefs. Show me someone who is sick and yet happy; in danger and yet happy; dying and yet happy; condemned to exile and yet happy; lost his reputation and yet happy. Show him to me, by god, I long to see a Stoic!

You may say that you don't know anyone so perfectly formed. All right. Then show me someone who is on the way to becoming one, someone walking in the right direction. Do me a favour. Don't refuse this old man a sight he has never seen. And don't show me the golden and ivory idols of Zeus, Pheidias, or his Athena. Show me a living person with a soul that never criticizes god or fellow human beings ever again, whose wishes never fail to come true, who never falls into anything he wants to avoid, who is never angry, envious, or jealous, and who desires to be god-like instead of just being human. A person, though in this lifeless body, is in communion with god. Show him to me. You cannot, can you? So why kid yourself and delude others? Why assume an identity that doesn't belong to you? You are like thieves who take clothes and property that don't belong to them.

[*Source*: *Discourses* II.19, 23-28]

---

78. Don't try to things beyond your means

Don't undertake to do things beyond your means. If you do, you will not only embarrass yourself but you will also miss an opportunity to successful things that are within your means.

[*Source*: *Enchiridion* 37]

---

79. Don't complain

You have been fighting with your help at home. Your household is a mess. You have disturbed your neighbours' peace. Now you have come here looking all dignified and scholarly. And you see fit to pass judgement on how I explain a text and say whatever nonsense that comes to my head?

You have come here in a spirit of envy because you get no allowance from home. You sit through my lectures and discussions while thinking all the while about how things are between you and your father or brother. "What are they saying about me back home? I suppose I am making progress and they are saying, 'He will come back knowing everything.' At one point, I suppose, I had hoped I would know everything. But that is hard work and I get no help from home. The baths here are awful. Things are going badly for me both at home and here."

Then people start saying that one is no better off for attending school. Who – I repeat who – goes to school to become a better person? Who goes to have their judgments examined, fully aware that they need to be examined? Is it any wonder you go back home with the same set of ideas that you came here with? You did not come here to have your ideas examined. Not in the least. Far from it. So at least think about this. Are you getting what *you* came here for? You want to chatter about philosophical principles. Well, aren't you getting better at that? Haven't you become more talkative than you were before? Aren't these topics that give you enough material for you to impress others? Haven't you learned logic and how to analyse an argument? Haven't you learned assumptions in *The Liar* and other hypothetical arguments?

"Why then are you unhappy, even though you got everything you came here for?"

[*Source*: *Discourses* II.21, 11-16]

80. Arouse others' desire to talk to you

Someone said to Epictetus:

"I have come to you many times, wanting to listen to you. But you have never given me an answer. But now, if possible, please say something to me."

"Do you think that there is an art to speaking with skill? If you don't possess this skill you will speak unskilfully?"

"I believe so, yes."

"Someone whose speech benefits oneself and others would be speaking with skill, and someone whose speech harms oneself and others would be speaking unskilfully. You would find that some suffer harm and others gain benefit. Do all listeners gain benefit from what they hear, or some gain benefit while others suffer harm?"

"Not all would gain benefit."

"Skilful listeners benefit and unskilful listeners are harmed?"

"Yes."

"Just as there is a skill in speaking, there is a skill in listening?"

"It would seem so."

"Consider it from another point of view, if you please. Whose job it is to play a musical instrument according to the rules of music?"

"The musician's."

"All right. Whose job is it to make a statue properly?"

"The sculptor's."

"Don't you think that it requires skill also to appreciate the statue properly?"

"Yes, it does."

Don't you see then, if speaking properly demands a skilled person, to listen with benefit also demands a skilled person? For the time being, let's not worry about what will eventually benefit us. After all, both of us are far removed from that question. But here is something that everyone could agree on. To listen to philosophers, it takes a great deal of practice in listening. Is this not true?

"What should I talk to you about, then? Tell me, what are you capable of hearing about? About what is good and evil? The good and evil of what? Maybe a horse?"

"No."

"Of an ox?"

"No."

"Of a human being?"

"Yes."

Do we know what a human being is? What his nature is? What the concept a human being is? Do we have ears sufficiently open with regard to this? Do you even have an idea of what nature is? Are you, to any extent, capable of following me as I speak? Shall I demonstrate it for you? How can I? Do you understand at all what proof is, what demonstration is, and how a proof is demonstrated? What looks like proof, but is not? Can you tell the difference between what is true and what is false? ... What I can do to get you excited about philosophy? ... So, show me what I can accomplish by talking to you. Kindle a desire in me. When a sheep sees grass, it kindles a desire in the sheep to eat, but not if you offer it a stone or a loaf of bread. Similarly some of us have a desire to speak if we come across a suitable listener who herself kindles such a desire. But if she sits like a stone, or grass, how can she kindle any such a desire? Does the vine say to the farmer "Look at me?" But it shows by the way it looks that anyone who cares for it will profit from it and so invites them to take care of it.

Which of us turn down the invitation of charming little children to join in their games, crawl with them, and engage in baby talk? But who wants to play with a donkey and bray like it? Even if it is little, a donkey is a donkey.

"Why don't you say anything to me then?"

I have only this to say to you. Anyone who is ignorant of who they are, what they are born for, in what kind of world they find themselves in and whom they share it with; who does not know what things are good and bad, what are honourable and shameful; who is unable to follow argument or proof, and cannot tell the difference between what is true and what is false: such a person will exercise neither their desires, nor aversions, nor impulses, nor choices in accordance with nature. Being deaf and blind, they would go around thinking they are somebody, while they are nobody in reality.

Is there anything new in all this? Hasn't this been so since the human race began? Isn't this ignorance the cause of all our errors and misfortunes? ...

This is all I have to say to you. And even this, with reluctance."

"Why do you say that?"

"Because you haven't kindled my enthusiasm. What can I see in you that makes me comparable to a rider seeing a thoroughbred horse? Your poor body? You have treated it in a shameful way. Your clothes? Too luxurious. Your bearing and looks? Not worth a second glance."

When you want to hear a philosopher, don't say, "Have you nothing to say to me?" Instead, show that you are capable of listening to the philosopher. You will then see then how you excite the speaker to talk to you.

[*Source: Discourses* II.24, abbreviated]

81. Your good depends on your choice

So, when you see friends or siblings who seem to be of one mind, don't rush to say anything about their friendship. Not even if they swear to it and say it is impossible to separate them. You cannot trust a bad person's judgement. It's weak, unstable, and readily influenced by one impression after another.

Don't simply ask, as others do, "Do they share the same parents?" or, "Did they grow up together?" or, "Did they go to the same school?" Just ask where they put their self-interest – things outside of themselves or in their power to choose? If their self-interest lies in external things, don't call them friends any more than you would call them trustworthy, consistent, determined, or free. No, don't even call them human beings, if you are wise... But if you hear that they sincerely believe that good lies with what is in their choice and where impressions are used correctly, then don't bother to find out if they belong to the same family or are long-term friends, even if it is the only thing you know about them. You can be confident that they are friends, fair and reliable. Where else can you find friendship if not with fairness, reliability and respect for what is honourable – and these things only? [*Source*: *Discourses* II.22, 24-27 and 29-30]

---

82. No one can rob us of our choice

No one can rob us of our choice or be a master of it. [*Source*: *Discourses* III.22, 105]

---

83. Until the end, take care of what you control

As far as I am concerned, when death finds me, I would rather be doing nothing other than taking care of things under the area of my choice – trying to make it unhindered, unrestrained, serene and free. I want to be able to say to God, "Have I in any way disobeyed your commands? Did I ever misuse the resources you gave me for any other purpose? Did I misuse my senses or my preconceptions? Did I ever accuse you of anything or find fault with the way you governed? I fell sick and it was your will. So did others, but I did it willingly. I became poor, it was your wish but I was joyful. I didn't hold any office because it was not your wish but I didn't set my heart on it. Have you ever seen me dejected because of it? Have I not always come before you with a cheerful face, prepared to do whatever you order me? Now it is your wish that I leave this festival. I go; full of gratitude to you that you found me worthy of sharing this festival with you; and see your works and the way you govern."

Let these be my thoughts, let this be my writing, and let this be my reading, when I face death.

[*Source: Discourses* III.5, 7-11]

84. Never accuse or blame anyone

Does it mean nothing to you to never to accuse anyone, never to blame anyone, be it God or men? To always have the same expression in one's face, coming in or going out? These are things that Socrates knew. Yet he never said he knew. He didn't teach either... Who, among you, makes the purpose of Socrates the purpose of your life? If you did, you would be glad to be ill, to go hungry, or to die. If anyone of you has been in love with a pretty woman, you will know that I am telling the truth.

[*Source: Discourses* III.5, 16-18 abbreviated]

85. Be free, high-minded and self-respecting

"What is in accordance with nature?"

"To be free, noble and self-respecting."

After all, what other animal blushes? What other animal has a sense of shame? It is our nature to subject pleasure to these considerations as their servant. This will arouse our interest in continuing to act in accordance with nature.

[*Source: Discourses* III.7, 27-28]

86. Your mind is your raw material

The human body is the raw material for the physician and physiotherapist. Land is the raw material for the farmer. The raw material for good human beings is their own mind

[Source: Discourses III.3, 1]

87. Don't be vengeful

Which one of you doesn't admire what the Spartan Lycurgus said when was blinded in one eye by a young citizen of Sparta? People turned him over to Lycurgus for punishment, the way he saw fit. Lycurgus not only did not take revenge but actually educated the youth and made a good man out of him and presented him at the theatre.

The Spartans were outraged, but Lycurgus said, 'You gave me a violent and aggressive person. I am returning him as a civilized and refined person.'

[Source Fragment. (Stobaeus); Schweigh lxvii; Shenckl 5]

88. Good attracts you soul, bad repulses it

A banker or a retailer cannot refuse to accept legal currency. They are obliged to accept it, whether they like it or not, in exchange for goods of equal value. So it is with the soul. When you present it with something good, it immediately moves towards it and it is repelled by anything bad. The soul will never reject a clear impression of good, any more than you would reject legal currency. Every action of God and humans are solely based on this principle.

[*Source*: *Discourses* III.3, 3-4]

89. 'General' and 'technical' perceptions

"Epictetus, what is 'general perception'?"

"When you hear a sound, it is general hearing. But when you distinguish between musical notes, it is no longer 'general,' but technical. There are things that people who are not altogether perverted can see because of their general faculties. Such mental condition is called 'general perception.'"

[*Source*: *Discourses* III.6, 8]

90. Be an example to others

Can you judge people?... Like Socrates, make us admire and imitate you. He was one person who governed people as human beings – he caused people to subject to him their desires and aversions and their impulses to act or not to act. "Do this; don't do that or I will send you to prison" is not the way to govern people as rational beings. No. What you should be saying is

"Do this in accordance with nature, or you will be punished, you will be harmed."

"Harmed in what way?"

"Only in this way: You will destroy yourself as a person of good faith, honour and decent behaviour. Look for no greater harm than that."

[*Source*: *Discourses* III.7, 30-36 Abbreviated]

91. Don't' add your judgement to reality

"His son is dead."

"What happened?"

"His son is dead."

"Nothing more?"

"Nothing more."

"The ship is lost."

"What happened?"

"The ship is lost."

"He was taken to prison."

"What happened?"

"He was taken to prison."

"It is too bad for him," is a comment that we add on our own. Yet, you may say, God is being unfair in all this. How so? Because he made you patient and high-minded? Because he prevented these things from being evil? Because he made it possible for you to suffer and still be happy? Or because he left the door open for you to use when what happens doesn't suit you? Go out, friend, and stop complaining.

[*Source*: *Discourses* III.8, 5-6]

92. Ever been on a journey of self-examination?

You are not content to stay home with the honours you have already received and you travel to Rome in order to receive the new honour of becoming a patron of the city. You desire something greater and more prominent. So, tell me, have you ever been on a journey to examine your own judgements so you can reject those that are unsound? Whom did you consult for that purpose? What time have you set aside for this? In what stage of your life? Run through those periods in your life. Do it in your mind, if you are ashamed to do it in front of me.

- Did you examine your life when you were a child? Isn't it true that what you were doing then was not different from what you are doing now?
- Did you examine your life when you were a young person? When you listened to those who taught rhetoric and practised it yourself, did you imagine that you were deficient in anything?
- Did you examine your life when you became a man and took part in public affairs? When you pleaded cases yourself and acquired a reputation, did you imagine anyone else could be your equal? Would you have tolerated it if someone tried to cross-examine you, to show that your judgments were bad?

"Help me with this."

"I have no rules to offer you on this. If you have come to me for that purpose, you should have come here intending to meet a philosopher rather than a greengrocer or a shoemaker, as you have done now."

"For what purpose, then, do philosophers offer rules?"

"For this purpose: Whatever happens, our ruling faculty continues to be in accordance with nature. Does this seem small to you?"

"No. It's of the greatest importance."

"Well, can that be completed in a short time, in a brief visit? If it can be so completed, do so. And then you will go away and complain, 'I met Epictetus, but it was like meeting with a stone or a statue.' Yes, you simply saw me, nothing more."

You meet someone properly as a person only when you understand his judgments and show him yours in turn. Discover my judgments, show me yours, and then you can say you have met me. Let us cross-examine each other. If any of my judgements is bad, take it away; if you any of yours is bad, let's bring it to light. This is what meeting a philosopher is all about.

But no, this is your way: "We were passing through. And, while we were waiting to charter a ship to go to Rome, we thought we could visit Epictetus to see what he has to say." Then you leave saying, "Epictetus was nothing at all. He murdered the language and spoke utter nonsense." What else could you judge, if you came here like this?

[*Source*: *Discourses* III.9, 6-14 abbreviated]

93. Better judgment makes a better person

"Whether you wish it not, you are poorer than I am."

"What do *I* need, then?"

"Things you don't have now: stability, a mind in accord with nature, and freedom from tension. Patron or no patron, what do I care? But *you* do. I am richer than you are. I am not anxious about what Caesar will think of me. I flatter no one for that purpose. This is what I have instead of your plates of gold and silver."

You may own gold wares, but your reasoning, your judgments and assent, your impulses and desires are earthenware.

[*Source: Discourses* III.9, 16-18]

94. Drop your desires

To you, all you have seems small. To me, all I have seems important. Your desires cannot be fulfilled. Mine already are. When children put their hands into narrow-necked jar to get nuts and figs out, the same thing happens. Once they fill their hand, they cannot get it out. They cry. Drop a few and you will easily get it out. You too should drop your desires. Don't set your heart upon too many things and you'll get what you want.

[*Source: Discourses* III.9, 21-22]

95. Forgiveness is better than revenge

Pittacus, wronged by one whom he had the power to punish, let him go free, saying, "Forgiveness is better than revenge." The one shows native gentleness, the other savagery. [Pittacus was one of the seven wise men of Greece and ruled Mytilene in Lesbos in the seventh century BCE.]

[*Source* Fragment. (Stobaeus); Schweigh lxviii]

96. What others do is their business

"My brother shouldn't have treated me this way."

"Quite so. But it is for him to see to that. No matter how he treats you, you need to conduct yourself the right way towards him. This is your business and not the rest. This no one can stop you from doing, while the other is open to hindrance.

[*Source: Discourses* III.10, 19-20]

97. Be self-sufficient and learn to live with yourself

Nevertheless, we should prepare ourselves to be self-sufficient and be able to live with ourselves. Even God lives with himself, converses with himself, thinks about the rules by which he governs the universe, and thinks thoughts that are worthy of him. Shouldn't we also be able to converse with ourselves, be self-sufficient, and know how to occupy ourselves? We should reflect on the divine governing order in our relationship to other things. We should consider how we used to respond to events and how we respond to them now, what things still bother us, and how to fix or remove them. If any of these need perfecting, we must perfect them in accordance with reason.

[*Source: Discourses* III.13, 6-8]

---

98. Until you become strong, be selective about who associate with

If you associate with others on a regular basis – for small talk, for parties, or for friendship – you will necessarily grow up to be like them, unless you get them to be like you. If you place a dead coal by a live one, either the live coal will set fire to the dead one or the dead coal will put out the live one. Since the stakes are high, you should be careful about socializing with lay people. Remember, it is impossible to rub against someone covered with dirt and avoid getting dirty yourself. What will you do if they talk about gladiators, horses, and sport heroes? Or worse, gossip about others – "So-and-so is good and so-and-so is bad; this is well done and that's done poorly"? Or if they taunt you, ridicule you, or even be of an ill-nature?

Do any of you have the ability of the musician who can pick up an instrument, identify right away which strings are out of tune, and so bring the whole instrument into tune? Or the ability of Socrates, who could win over the company to his side in every conversation? How could you? Most likely, you are going to adopt their mentality.

Why are they stronger than you? Because they talk their nonsense with conviction while your fine points come out of your lips. Your talk has no vigour, no life. It will turn people's stomachs to hear you go on and on about your miserable "virtue." So they get the better of you. Conviction is all-powerful and irresistible. So until these fine points take firm root in you and you can start relying on them safely, I advise you to be careful in associating with such people.

[*Source*: *Discourses* III.16, 1-8]

99. Train your mind like you train your body

All training applied to exercising the body may also be usefully applied to desires and aversions. But if they are directed towards showing off, it is a sign that you have turned to externals, hunting for some other victim and are seeking for an audience to applaud you, "What a great person!"

Thus, [the philosopher] Apollonius was right when he used to say, "If you want to train for your own sake, then, when you are thirsty in hot weather, take sip of cold water into your mouth and then spit it out. Don't tell anyone about it."

[*Source*: *Discourses* III.12, 16-17]

100. Practice deprivation

Practice one time living like someone who is ill, so you can live like a healthy person in another. Take no food, just drink water. Abstain from every desire at one time so as to be able to exercise your desires in a reasonable way at a later time.

[*Source*: *Discourses* III.13, 21]

101. Be a model for others to follow

Do you want to help them? Then show them by your own example the kind of person philosophy produces. Stop talking nonsense.

• Bring benefit to those who eat with you, by the way in which you eat.

• Bring benefit to those who drink with you, by the way in which you drink.

• Help them by yielding to them, by giving way to them, and not showering them with your spittle!

[*Source*: *Discourses* III.13, 23]

102. Don't hide, be open

Bad choral singers cannot sing on their own, but only with many others. Likewise, some people cannot walk on their own. If you are anyone at all, walk on your own, talk to yourself and do not hide yourself in the chorus. Put up with being laughed at sometimes. Look around you and shake yourself up to learn who you are.

[*Source*: *Discourses* III.14, 1-3]

103. Consider what's involved before jumping in

"I want to win at the Olympics."

Yes, but consider what comes first and what comes after and then, if it is to your advantage, set to work. You must accept the discipline, submit to the diet, stay away from pastries, train as you are ordered at the appointed time, in heat or cold. You must not drink cold water or wine as you like. In short, you should hand yourself to your trainer as you would to a doctor.

Then, when the time for the contest arrives you have to compete in digging [*the practice of covering yourself with mud before a wrestling match*], sometimes dislocate your wrist, sprain your ankle, and swallow quantities of sand and get whipped. And then, get defeated sometimes – after all that! Reflect on these things. Then, if you still want to become an athlete, go for it.

Otherwise, know that you are behaving like children who sometimes play wrestlers, sometimes gladiators, sometimes blow a trumpet, and then play act whatever they have seen and admired. Likewise, you're an athlete sometimes, gladiator sometimes; now a philosopher and then an orator; but nothing wholeheartedly. Like an ape, you imitate whatever you see. One thing after another catches your fancy, but it stops pleasing you, once you become familiar with it. You have never started on anything with enough consideration, have never examined the entire thing carefully and systematically, but have always approached things randomly and half-heartedly.... But first consider what you are taking on, then your own nature, and what you can endure. If you want to be a wrestler, you will have to look to your shoulders, your back and your thighs. For different people are made for different things.

Do you think you can act the way you do and yet become a philosopher? That you can eat and drink like you do now, and be angry and irritable? You must stay up at night, you must work hard, overcome certain desires, abandon your people, be scorned by a slave, laughed at by those who meet you; come off worse than others in everything: in office, in honour, and in the courts. When you have considered all these drawbacks carefully, if you still think it fit, then approach philosophy. Be willing to give up all of this in exchange for serenity, freedom, and peace of mind.

[*Source*: *Discourses* III.15, 2-7 and 9-12]

104. Don't be a child uneducated in the art of living

After all, it is being a child to be uncultivated in matters of culture, unschooled in matters of literature, and uneducated in matters relating to the art of living.

[*Source*: *Discourses* III.19, 6]

105. You can benefit from everything

"Is it possible, then, to benefit from these things?"

"Yes, from everything."

"Even from someone who insults me?"

"What advantage does a wrestler get from his sparring partner? The greatest. Well, the person who insults you is your sparring partner. He trains you in patience, in being free of anger, and in gentleness."

You disagree. Yet the man who grips your neck and gets your hips and shoulders in shape brings you benefit ... Yet you say that one who trains you in being free of anger brings you no benefit. It is simply you don't know how to draw benefit from other people.

Your neighbour is bad? Bad to himself, but good to you.

This is the magic wand of Hermes [son of Zeus]: As the saying goes, "Touch what you like, it will turn into gold." For me, bring me anything and I'll turn it into something good. Bring sickness, death, poverty, abuse, or even a trial for your own life. All these, under the touch of the wand of Hermes, will become a source of benefit.

[*Source*: *Discourses* III.20, 9-12 abbreviated]

106. Be careful about your associates, until your principles are firmly rooted

So until these fine points take firm root in you and you can start relying on them safely, I advise you to be careful in associating with such people. Otherwise, whatever you write down here will melt away like wax in the sun. As long as your opinions are merely like wax, keep well out of the sun.

[*Source*: *Discourses* III.16, 9-10]

107. Be aware of your limitations

You need to approach this very differently. This is a great mission, a serious mystery and is not granted to anyone who comes along. Even being wise may not be enough to take care of the young. You should have a special aptitude and inclination and, by God, a particular physique. You need a calling from God to fulfil this function, just as Socrates was called to fulfil the function of correcting errors of others, as

Diogenes was called to fulfil the function of regally reprimanding them, and as Zeno was called to fulfil the function of teaching and establishing the principles of philosophy.

Instead, you want to start practicing as a doctor, having nothing more than your medicines. You neither know nor have taken the time to learn when and how you should apply them.

[*Source*: *Discourses* III.21, 17-20]

108. You're not a philosopher, unless you practice philosophy

If philosophical principles interest you, sit down and work on them yourself. But don't say that you are a philosopher and don't let anyone else say that you are one. Say instead, "He is mistaken. My desires are not different from what they were before, nor are they directed towards other things. I don't assent to other things than what I used to. And I am not able to interpret impressions any better."

[*Source*: *Discourses* III.21, 23]

109. You need to be blessed to be a philosopher

One of his students who was attracted to Cynicism asked Epictetus,

"Who is qualified to be a Cynic?"

"Let us examine the idea at length," said Epictetus.

But first let me tell you this much. If someone attempts to understand this great topic while not believing in God or hating him, it is nothing but a disgraceful behaviour in front of the public. In a well-managed house, not anyone can declare, "I should be running this place." If you do, the master of the house will see you giving orders and you will be dragged and thrown out. It is so with this world too. For here is a master of the house who orders everything. He says,

"You are the sun. Go round and make the year and season. Make the fruits and nourish them. Stir the winds and make them calm. Warm people's bodies. Go, travel around, and manage things from the greatest to the least."

"You are cow. When a lion appears, run away. If you don't, you'll suffer."

"You are a bull. Step forward and fight the lion, because this is your business. It becomes you and you can do it.

"You are capable of leading an army against Troy. Be Agamemnon."

"You are capable of fighting against Hector in a single combat. Be Achilles."

But if [the inferior fighter] Thersites had come forward to claim the command, he wouldn't have got it. If he had, he would have disgraced himself in front of several witnesses.

[*Source: Discourses* III.22, 1-8]

---

110. Honour is the only protection for a philosopher

You should know that, when people do things of this nature, they are protected by walls, houses, and darkness. They have much to conceal. A man shuts the doors, stations someone outside his bedroom and says, "If someone comes calling say, 'He's out, he is busy.'"

Instead of all this, a Cynic uses only his honour as his protection. If he doesn't, he himself will be indecent when he is naked under the open sky. Honour is his house, his door, his doorkeeper and his darkness.

[*Source: Discourses* III.22, 14-15]

111. Wherever you go, there will be sun

Death? Let death come whenever it chooses, either to the whole body or a part. 'Fly,' you say. And to where? Can you banish me from this universe? You cannot. But, wherever I go, there will be Sun, there will be moon, there will be stars, dreams, prophesies, and conversation with gods."

[*Source: Discourses* III.22, 21]

112. Be a spy – look for what's good and what's bad

[The true Cynic] must know that he has been sent by God to be a messenger to people about good and bad things. To show them that they have wandered and are looking for the nature of good and bad in the wrong places, rather than where it really is.

After the battle of Chaeronea, Diogenes was brought to Philip. A Cynic is indeed a spy – a spy of what is good and what is bad. It is his duty to examine carefully and report accurately thus: not to be struck with terror because there are no enemies, not to be confused in any other way by impressions.

[*Source*: *Discourses* III.22, 23-25]

113. You can have nothing, and yet be free

"But if someone has nothing – no clothes, no home or fireplace, no clean place, no one who would assist, no city – how is it possible for a person like that to be happy?"

"God has sent us someone like that to show that it is indeed possible. 'Look at me. I have no country, no home, no possessions, and no servants. I sleep on the ground. I don't have a wife or children or fine residence, just earth and sky and one sorry cloak. And what do I lack? Am I not without sorrow, without fear? Am I not free? Have you even seen me fail to get what I want or get what I try to avoid? Have I ever blamed God or another human being? Have I ever yelled at anyone? Have you ever seen me with a sad face? How do I treat people whom you fear and stand in awe of? Do I not treat them as if they were slaves? As a matter of fact, whenever they see me, they treat me as their lord and master.'

[*Source*: Discourses III.22, 45-49]

114. Know your limits

Think more carefully, know your limits, don't go forward without the help of God.

[*Source*: Discourses III.22, 53]

115. A philosopher contributes to the society in a different way

"But, can a Cynic choose to marry and have children?"

"In a city of sages, it is quite possible that no one would live the life of a Cynic. For whose sake would he do it? But, supposing there is a Cynic there, then nothing would prevent him from marrying and having children. His wife and her father would be like him, his children would be brought up to be like him. But now everything is ordered now as though for a battle. Isn't it necessary that a Cynic be free from distraction, dedicated to his sacred ministry, ready to walk around? If he is tied down to private obligations and mixed up in relationships that he cannot very well ignore, can he still maintain his character as a wise and good man? If he remains faithful to them, will it not destroy his nature as a messenger and spy carrying a divine message?"

[*Source*: *Discourses* III.22, 67-69] 116

116. A philosopher is engaged in public life

Go on and ask me if a Cynic will engage in public affairs. Tell me, you fool, what public affair are you looking for other than the one he is engaged in right now? Or should he come forward and give speeches to his fellow citizens about revenues and taxes when his business is to talk to the entire humankind – not about debits and credits or war and peace – but about happiness and unhappiness, good fortune and bad, slavery and freedom? You are asking me if someone will engage in public affairs when he is already engaged in it in such a big way. Ask me too whether he will accept public office. I will tell you, "What office, you fool, is greater than the one he has now?"

[*Source*: *Discourses* III.22, 83-85]

117. A philosopher should look after their bodies too

A Cynic's body, however, should be in good shape. His philosophy will not carry much conviction if it comes from a sickly, thin, and pale body. It is not enough for him to prove to ordinary people, through constancy of his mind, that it is possible to be good and noble without the material things they value. He also has to show, by his body, that a plain and simple outdoor life is wholesome: 'See, both I and my body testify.' This was so with Diogenes. He walked about with radiant health and would draw the attention of the crowd by it. But a Cynic who aroused pity seems like a beggar. People avoid him and are offended by him. He should not be dirty and thus scare away people. Even his ruggedness should be clean and engaging.

[*Source*: *Discourses* III.22, 86-89]

118. A philosopher's conscience is the source of their authority

Even corrupt kings and tyrants, because they have weapons and bodyguards, can reprimand and punish wrongdoers. A Cynic derives the same authority of weapon and bodyguards through his conscience. He knows he has watched over others and worked on their behalf. His sleep is pure and he wakes up even purer. His thoughts were of a friend and servant of the gods and he shares in the governance of gods and ready to say under all conditions,

"Lead me Zeus; and thou, O Destiny,"

and

"If this what pleases the gods, so be it."

Why then, should such person not speak boldly to his brothers? To his children? In a word, his own relations?

[*Source: Discourses* III.22, 94-96] 119

---

119. A philosopher does not invite followers, he attracts them

But does a philosopher invite people to a lecture? Like the sun which draws nourishment to itself, a philosopher attracts people in need of help. What doctor would ever invite patients so he can treat him? (Although, now I hear that in Rome even doctors advertise for patients. In my time, they were called in by patients.)

"I invite you to come and hear how unwell you are:
You take care of everything except what you should;
You don't know good from evil; and
You are unfortunate and unhappy."

A charming invitation! Yet, unless a philosopher produces this effect through his speech, it is lifeless and so is the philosopher.

[*Source: Discourses* III.23, 27-28] 120

120. The school of philosophy is like a hospital

The school of a philosopher is a hospital. When you leave, you should leave in pain, not pleasure. You were not healthy when you came in. You had a dislocated shoulder, or an abscess, or a fistula, or a headache. So am I supposed to sit down with you and recite with your pretty thoughts and reflections so you go away praising me, but with the same dislocated shoulder, the same abscess, the same fistula, or the same headache that you came with? And is it for this that young people should travel abroad, leaving their parents, friends, relations and possessions behind, so they can say, "Bravo!" as you deliver your clever phrases?

[*Source*: *Discourses* III.23, 30-31]

121. You are not made to be unhappy

If someone is unhappy, remember, they are responsible for it. God made us humans to be happy and serene.

[*Source*: *Discourses* III.24, 2]

122. Things change

Shouldn't we, once and for all, wean ourselves and remember what we learned from philosophers, unless we listened to them merely as story-tellers? They said that this universe is just a single city; it is made of a single thing. There must be a change from time to time when one thing gives way to another, some things disappear and other things come into being, somethings remain and other things are moved somewhere else.

The world is full of friends, first the gods and then human beings, who by nature are endeared to each other.

[*Source*: *Discourses* III.24, 9-11]

123. Be happy wherever you are

Considering that [Odysseus left these children as orphans without lamentation and regret? He knew that no human being is an orphan but there's a father who constantly cares for them all. Because for him it was not just idle talk that Zeus is the father of human beings, but he always thought of him as his own father, and called him so, and looked to him in all that he did. That's why he could live happily wherever he was.

[*Source*: *Discourses* III.24, 15-16] 124

124. Your life is a battle

Don't you know that this life is like a campaign? One person should guard, another go on a spying mission, and yet another out to fight. All of them cannot be in the same place and it wouldn't be desirable either. But you neglect to perform the job assigned to you by the general, complain that it is hard, and don't realize how you are reducing the army to the extent you can. For, if others follow your example, no one will dig a trench, or build a fence, no one will keep watch at night, or expose himself to danger – they will all be useless as soldiers ... So it is here. Everyone's life is a campaign, long and changeable. You must fulfil the duty of a soldier and do whatever your general orders you to do, sometimes even divining his wishes. For, he is no ordinary general, either in power or excellence of character.

[Source: Discourses III.24, 31-32, 34-35]

125. Do things because they are right

"What, have you forgotten why you went there? Don't you know that wise and good people do things because they are right and not because they look good to others?" ...

"No further reward to be gained, then?"

"Why do you seek further rewards for a good person than doing what is wise and right? At the Olympics, you don't ask for anything further than the Olympic crown. Does it look too small and worthless to you to be good, noble, and happy?

[Source: Discourses III.24, 50-53 abbreviated]

126. Don't be unhappy because of someone else

We should not be unhappy because of someone else, but we should be happy for all, most of all for God, who made us for this purpose.

[Source: Discourses III.24, 63]

127. Be kind-hearted and gentle

What! Was there anyone at all whom Diogenes didn't love? Was he not so gentle and kind-hearted that he gladly took upon himself so many troubles and physical hardships for the common good of humanity?

"But in what way did he show his love?"

"By taking good care of others while being obedient to God, as a servant of God,"

[*Source*: *Discourses* III.24, 64]

128. You are born for what is good

I am born for what is good and what belongs to me, not for what is evil.

[*Source*: *Discourses* III.24, 83]

129. Remember, people you love are mortal

You should remind yourself that what you love is mortal. What you love is not your own. It has been given to you for the time being, not permanently, not forever. Rather it is given to you like fig or a bunch of grapes, for a particular season of the year....

"But these are words can bring bad luck."....

Do you call anything bad luck except what indicates something bad for us? Cowardice, meanness of spirit, sorrow, and shamelessness – all these are words of bad luck. And yet, we should not avoid using them, if they will protect us from the things themselves.

Are you telling me that any word that signifies some process of nature is bad luck? Is it bad luck for corn to be harvested because corn is destroyed? Is it bad luck for leaves to fall, or for a fresh fig to turn into a dried one, or for grapes to turn into raisin? All these things involve changes from their former state to a new and different one. It is not destruction but an orderly management and organization. Travelling abroad is like that, a small change. Death is like that, a big change, a change from what is into what it *presently* is not (rather than what is not).

"So I won't exist anymore?"

You won't exist, but something else that the world needs will. You did not come into being when you wanted to, but when the world had a need for you.

[*Source: Discourses* III.24, 86 and 89-94 abbreviated]

---

130. Leave the world as a free person

A wise and good person, keeping in mind who she is, and where she came from and who created her, thinks about one thing only: how to fulfil her place in a disciplined manner, remaining obedient to God.

"Is it your will that I continue to live? I'll live as a free and noble person as you wish me to be. You have made me free from hindrance in all things that are my own. Now you don't have any further need for me? May all be well with you. I have remained here so far only because of you and no other. Now I obey you and leave.

"How do you leave?"

"Again as you wish. As a free person, as your servant, taking note of your commands and your prohibitions.

[*Source: Discourses* III.24, 95-98]

131. If you can't live in accordance with nature, then God is signalling you to leave

Whatever place or position you give me, as Socrates says, I'll die a thousand times rather than abandon it."

Where do you want me to be? In Rome, Athens, Thebes, or Gyara? Only remember me there. If you send me to a place where it is impossible to live in accordance with nature, I shall depart from this life. Not out of disobedience to you, but in the belief that you are giving me the signal to leave. I'm not abandoning you, heaven forbid! But I realize you have no further need for me.

[*Source*: *Discourses* III.24, 99-101]

132. A wise person knows how act with discipline

If you are in Gyara, don't picture how it was in Rome, what pleasures you enjoyed there and what pleasures await you there if you go back. Since Gyara is where you are now, you should live boldly there, as is proper for someone who lives there. And if you are in Rome, don't imagine the way of life in Athens, but think only about how best live where you are.

Finally, in place of all other pleasures, think of the ones that come from the awareness that you are obeying God and that you are playing the part of a good and excellent person,

[*Source*: *Discourses* III.24, 109-110]

133. Nothing bad happens to a good person

Nothing bad ever happens to a good person, either in life or in death.

"Yes, but what if he fails to provide me with food?"

"What else? Like a good general, he is signalling you to withdraw."

I came into this world when it pleased him and leave it again at his pleasure. While I lived, it was my job to sing hymns of his praise to myself or to others, one or many.

[*Source: Discourses* III.26, 28-30]

134. The source of all evils is not death, but the fear of death

Why don't you realize then that the source of all human evils, mean-spiritedness, and cowardice is not death itself but the fear of death? Train yourself to face this. You should direct all your reasoning, all your studies and all your exercises towards this end. Then you will know that it is the only way for you to achieve freedom.

[*Source: Discourses* III.26, 38-39]

135. You're free when you live as you please

You are free when you live as you wish; when you cannot be compelled, obstructed, or controlled; your choices cannot be blocked; when you get your desires fulfilled, and when you don't face anything you want to avoid.

"Who wants to go through life, without knowing of how to achieve this?"

"No one."

"Who wants to be deceived, reckless, unjust, undisciplined, mean and ungrateful?"

"No one."

"So, no bad person lives the way they want. No bad person is free. Who wants to live in sorrow, fear, envy, and pity? Who wants to fail to get what they want and to get what they do not want?"

"No one."

"So, can we find a bad person free from fear, frustration, or misfortune?"

"No."

"So, we find no one who's free."

[*Source*: *Discourses* IV.1, 1-3]

---

136. Align your desires with reality

This is how cautious travellers act as well. When they hear that there are robbers along the way, they do not go off on their own but wait for a group of people who travel together and go with them. A sensible person will behave the same way in life, thinking, "There are many thieves and bandits, many storms and many chances to lose my valuable things. How can I be safe? How can I escape thieves and robbers? Who should I attach myself to? Some rich and powerful person? What good will it do me if he loses his position and breaks down? What if my travel companion himself turns against me and robs me? What should I do?" By thinking this way, the traveller concludes that if he allied himself with God he would safely complete his journey.

[*Source*: *Discourses* IV.1, 91-98]

137. Act the way God wants you to act

"What do you mean by 'allied himself to God'?"

"It means acting in such a way that whatever God wants, that is what we also want. If he doesn't want something, we don't want it either."

"How can we do this?"

"By paying attention to his purpose and design."

[*Source*: *Discourses* IV.1, 99-100]

138. Don't be upset when things are taken back

You have received everything – including your life – from your benefactor. Yet, you are angry with the giver for taking things back?

Who are you? Why did you come here? Isn't it God who brought you here? Hasn't he shown you the light? Hasn't he given you the people who support you? Hasn't he given you your senses? Hasn't he given you reason?

How did he bring you here? As a mortal, as one who would live here in flesh for a while, witness his grand design, and share briefly the pageant and the festival with him. So why not enjoy the feast and pageant while you are able? And when the time is up and when he leads you out, why not go out thanking him for what you have seen and heard?

"But I want to enjoy the festival a while longer."

"Yes. So would newcomers to mysteries – they would like the initiation ceremonies to continue. So would the Olympic crowd – they would like to see more contestants. But the festival is over. Discreetly move on. Be grateful for what you have seen."

[*Source*: *Discourses* IV.1, 103-106]

139. Appreciate it what you have, while you have it

Why are you so greedy and dissatisfied? Why do you crowd the world?

"Yes, but I want my wife and children with me."

"Why? Are they yours? Don't they belong to the one who gave them to you? The one who created you as well? Will you hang on to what's not yours and refuse to give them up? Do you want to challenge someone better?"

"Why did he bring me in this world with all these conditions attached?"

"If you don't like it, leave. He doesn't need fault finders. He needs those who are keen to join in the festival and the dance – those who would applaud the festival with their praise and acclaim. He wouldn't mind dismissing the grumpy and the cowardly."

Even when such people are invited, they don't act as though they are at a festival or play their proper role. Instead they whine, find fault with God, their fortune, and their fellow human beings. They don't appreciate their own powers and resources given to them for the opposite purpose – to be generous, high-minded, courageous, and free – exactly what we are talking about now.

[*Source*: *Discourses* IV.1, 106-109]

140. Be aware
where all good things come from

"Are *you* free then?"

"God, I wish and pray to be. But I still can't face my masters. I continue to value my body and try to keep it healthy, although it is hardly healthy. But if you want to see an example, I will point to Diogenes."

Diogenes was free. Why? Not because his parents were free because they weren't. He was free himself because he got rid of all handles of slavery. There was no way anyone could get close to him, capture him, and make him a slave. Everything he owned was only loosely tied to him. He could let go of everything. If you grabbed his property, he would rather let you have it than be pulled along with it. If you grabbed his leg, he would let go of his leg; if you grabbed hold his body, he would let go of his body. The same with family, friends, and country [the universe itself]. He was aware where they all came from, who gave them, and the conditions attached to them.

But he would never have given up his true parents [the gods] and his real country. He was more obedient to gods than anyone else. He was more willing to die for his country than anyone else. He didn't pretend to care for the world for show. He was constantly aware that everything that comes into being has a source. Things happen for the sake of the universe at the command of its governor.

[*Source*: *Discourses* IV.1, 151-155]

141. Philosophers don't act contrary to reason

Study these principles, these judgments, these arguments, and think about these examples. Does it come as a surprise to you that such a great goal needs many sacrifices? What people commonly consider as freedom, many had hanged themselves, thrown themselves over cliffs. Occasionally, even entire cities have been destroyed. So, for the sake of the true, secure, and unshakable freedom, will you not return to God what he gave you when he asks for it? As Plato says, be prepared not only to die but to be tortured, deported, beaten – in short, to give back everything that is not your own. Otherwise, you will be a slave among slaves – even if you are a consul a thousand times over, and even if you go up to the Palace – you will remain a slave all the same.

And you will see what Cleanthes meant when he said that, "Perhaps philosophers do things that are contrary to expectation, but not contrary to reason."

[*Source*: *Discourses* IV.1, 170-173]

142. Living nobly is the best revenge

When asked how one should best avenge an enemy, Epictetus replied, "By setting oneself to live the noblest life oneself."

[*Source* Fragment. (Antonius Monachus); Schweigh cxxx]

143. Whatever you do, guard your own good

I am a free man, a friend of God. I obey him of my own free will. But I should not lay claim to anything else – body, property, office, reputation – nothing, in short. God doesn't want me to claim these things either. If it was his desire, he would have made them good for me. He hasn't done so and I won't disobey his orders.

In everything you do, guard your own good. As for the rest, be happy to take things as they come and use them rationally. Otherwise you will have bad luck and no good luck, and you will be restrained and blocked. These are the laws that have been sent to you from above. These are the laws that you should interpret and obey, and not the laws of Masurius and Cassius. [Masurius and Cassius were distinguished jurists at that time.]

[Source: Discourses IV.3, 9-12]

---

144. True serenity is continuous and undisturbed

A desire for money and power makes you miserable and submissive to others. But so does its opposite, a desire for leisure, peace, travel, and learning. As a rule, if we attach value to externals of any kind, it would make us submissive to others. It makes little difference whether you *want* to be a senator or *not want* to be one; whether you *want* to hold office or *not* want to hold office; whether you say, "I'm in a bad way. I can't do anything because I am tied to books," or you say, "I'm in a bad way. I've no time to read." A book is external. So is a position external, like honour and office.

Why do you want to read anyway? For entertainment or to learn something? Either way, you are being frivolous and lazy. Judged by proper standards, reading should lead you to peace. If it doesn't, what good is it?

"But reading does make me peaceful. That's exactly why I am unhappy when I'm deprived of it."

"What kind of peace is this if it can be so easily disturbed? Not even by the Emperor or a friend of the Emperor but by a crow, a flute player, fever, or thirty thousand other things? True peace of mind is continuous and undisturbed."

[Source: Discourses IV.4, 1-5]

145. Act well today to make everyday a festival

If you have got rid of or reduced your tendency to impulsiveness, indecent language, recklessness, laziness, and if you are not motivated by the same things that motivated you once, at least not to the same extent, then everyday becomes a festival: today because you acted well yesterday, tomorrow because you acted well today.

How much better reason is this for thanksgiving than a consulship or a governorship!

[Source: Discourses IV.4, 46-47]

146. The source of all good things: You and God

These things come to you from your own self and from God. Remember who gave them, to whom, and why. If you are brought up to reason like this, how can you ever ask where you will be happy and where you will please God? No matter where they are, aren't people equally distant from God? And, no matter where they are, don't they all see the same thing?

[*Source*: *Discourses* IV.4, 47-48]

147. External things are not yours, and of no value to you

[Inward freedom] is a God-given right, free from restrictions.

Such judgments bring love to a household, harmony to a nation and peace among nations of the world. They make a person grateful to God and always confident, because what he is dealing with is not his own and, therefore, is of no value to him.

[*Source*: *Discourses* IV.5, 34-35]

148. While seeking the truth, don't be afraid you will be defeated

If you seek the truth, you will stop trying to gain victory by every possible means. When you find it, you need not fear being defeated.

[*Source* Fragment. Schweigh xxxix;
Shenkl *Gen. Epict. Stob.* 29]

149. If you have the right judgment, you will not be upset

What nonsense is this? How can I have right judgment when I am not satisfied with who I am but feel upset about how I look to others?

[*Source*: *Discourses* IV.6, 24] 150

150. Your good lies in things that are free

God made everything in the universe free from hindrance, self-sufficient, and every part of it serves the needs of the whole.

No other animal can understand nature's rule. But human beings are rational. They can think about these things and know that he is a part of them, the kind of part he is, and also to know it is all right for parts to work for the benefit of the whole. Human beings are noble by nature, high minded, and free rational animals. So, they notice that some things around them are free, unrestricted, and under their control, and others are not. What is within their control and choice is free and unrestricted. What is not within their choice and control is unfree and restricted.

Therefore, if you decide that your good and advantage lies only in things that are free and unrestricted and completely under your control, you will be free, peaceful, unharmed, high-minded, reverent, thankful to God for all things, never finding fault with anything or blaming anything.

On the other hand, if you decide that your good and advantage lie in external things that are outside you control, inevitably you will be hindered and restrained. You will be slavish to those who have control over the things that you so admire or fear. You will necessarily be disrespectful to God because you believe that He is harming you, unjust. You will be trying to claim more than your proper share and you are bound to become base and mean-spirited.

[Source: Discourses IV.7, 6-11]

151. Let what happens happen

Who can I be afraid of now? The officials? What could they do, shut the door on me? Let them shut the door, if I want to enter it."

"Then why do you come to the door?"

"Because I think it is fitting for me to take part in the game as long as it lasts."

"Why aren't you shut out?"

"Because, if I am shut out, I have desire to go in. I always want what actually happens. God's judgement is better than my desires. I am his servant, his follower. His choice is my choice. His desire is my desire. His will is my will. No one can shut me out. Only a person who tries to force their way in can be shut out."

[*Source*: *Discourses* IV.7, 19-20]

152. Grow better day-by-day

But what does Socrates say? :"One person finds pleasure in improving their land, another, their horses. My pleasure lies in seeking that myself grow better day by day."

[*Source*: *Discourses* III.5, 14]

153. Don't judge a book by its cover

No, they get their titles from their art, not from their clothes.

It is for this reason that [philosopher who dressed conventionally] Euphrates said,

"For a long time, I tried to hide the fact that I was a philosopher, and this worked for me. First, whatever I did, I did for my own sake and not for the sake of those watching me. It was for me that I ate properly, looked calm in the way I looked and moved. All this was for me and my God. Also, the contest was mine alone and so were the risks. If I did anything shameful or improper, it did not affect the cause of philosophy; I didn't commit faults as a philosopher. So those who did not know my intention used to wonder why I never became a philosopher, even though I knew all philosophers and lived with them. And where is the harm when people discover me as a philosopher because of what I do rather than by the way I dress?"

[*Source*: *Discourses* IV.8, 16-20]

154. Wait until it is time for you to bloom

Practice so you don't let people know who you are at first. Keep your philosophy to yourself for a while. This is how fruit is produced: the seed must be buried and hidden for a season; it must then grow slowly to perfection.

But if it heads out before the stalk is properly jointed, it never matures, as with the plants in a garden of Adonis. ["Plants in a garden of Adonis" is proverbial saying for incompleteness and early fading.] Now you are like this plant. You have bloomed before your time and will wither in winter.

[*Source*: *Discourses* IV.8, 35-37]

155. Destruction and deliverance come from within

First judge your actions. When you have condemned them, do not give up on yourself. Don't act like spiritless people who, once they give in, abandon themselves completely and are swept off by the current. Instead, learn from gymnastic trainers: Has the boy fallen down? "Get up and wrestle again until you get strong." You should also react in some similar way. You should know there is nothing more flexible than the human mind. You only to have to will a thing; it happens and it is set right. On the other hand, you only have to doze off and all is lost. Both destruction and deliverance come from within.

[*Source: Discourses* IV.9, 14-16]

156. Difficulties show what a person is made of

It is difficulties that show what a person is made of. So, when you face some difficulty, think of yourself as a wrestler. God, as your trainer, has matched you with a tough young opponent. But why? To turn you into Olympic-class material. This cannot be done without sweat.

[*Source: Discourses* I.24, 1-2]

157. Ignore what others think of you

To make progress, you should be able to accept being seen as ignorant or naïve. Don't strive to be thought of as wise. Even if you succeed in impressing others as a wise person, don't believe it yourself.

You cannot be in agreement with nature and, at the same time, care about things outside your control. Caring about one thing comes at the expense of caring for the other.

[Source: Enchiridion 13]

158. Be gentle in your dealings

Always conduct yourself as though you are at a formal dinner. If the dish has not reached you yet, don't be impatient. Wait your turn. When it comes around to you, reach out and take a modest amount. If it passes by you, don't try to pull it back.

If you act the same gentle and restrained way with your spouse, children, wealth, and status, you will be entitled to dine with the gods. If you go a step further and decline even what is given to you, you will not only be in the company of gods, but share their powers as well.

[Source: Enchiridion 15]

159. You are an actor in a play

Consider yourself as an actor in a play. The nature of the play – whether short or long – is for the director to decide. The director will also decide whether your role is one of a poor person, a rich person, a cripple, a king, or a commoner. You as an actor do not decide these things.

Like an accomplished actor you need to perform the role assigned to you in life skilfully. The responsibility for deciding what role you play rests with someone else.

[Source: Enchiridion 17]

160. You are an actor in a play

Whenever you face difficult situations in life, remember the prospect of death and other major tragedies that can and do happen to people. You will see that, compared to death, none of the things you face in life is important enough to worry about.

[*Source*: *Enchiridion* 21]

161. Evil is not intentional

No one sets up a target so others can miss it. Similarly, nature has not set up evil in this world so you can avoid it.

[*Source*: *Enchiridion* 27]

162. Piety is not different from self-interest

If a divine order exists, as it does, we should hold correct beliefs about it. The order governs the world well and is just. We are here to be in tune with the natural order of things and welcome whatever happens as the product of the highest intelligence. This way you will neither blame the divine order nor think that it does not exist.

But first you should stop applying labels like "good" and "bad" to what is not under your control. The labels good and bad apply only to things under your control. If you consider anything beyond your control as good or bad, you will fail to get what you want and get what you don't want. You will blame the divine order and think of it as the cause of your troubles

Everything in nature moves away from whatever is harmful and moves towards whatever is helpful. If you believe that someone has harmed you, you cannot love the offender or the offence. This is the reason why children who don't get what they want blame their parents, farmers curse the weather, and those who have lost their loved ones curse the gods.

Piety does not exist apart from self-interest. Therefore, when you practice using desire and aversion in the right way, you practice being pious.

Even so, it is never wrong to make sacrifice, offer drinks or other things to people, as long as it is done mindfully and not casually. Do not be miserly in your giving but be careful that you do not spend beyond your means either.

[*Source: Enchiridion* 31]

163. You are an actor in a play

Decide first what type of person you want to be and stick to it. Be the same person whether you are by yourself or with others. Here are some suggestions:

- Don't indulge in unnecessary chatter. Avoid gossiping about others. Speak with precision and speak about what really matters. In general, be silent
- If you want to influence your friends, do it by your example.
- If you find yourself cut off without escape in a conversation among strangers, be silent.

[*Source: Enchiridion* 33]

164. Don't be loud

Do not laugh too loud or too often.

[*Source*: *Enchiridion* 33]

165. You are an actor in a play

If possible, avoid taking oaths.

[*Source*: *Enchiridion* 33]

166 Avoid people who don't share your values

Avoid fraternizing with people who don't share your values. Prolonged association with those with false ideas can only tarnish your thinking.

[*Source*: *Enchiridion* 33]

167. Avoid showing-off

Be moderate in meeting the needs of your body, be it food, drink, clothing, shelter, or household needs. Avoid ostentation and luxury.

[*Source*: *Enchiridion* 33]

168. Don't be defensive

Don't defend yourself if someone speaks ill of you. Say instead "Obviously he didn't know my other faults, otherwise, he wouldn't have mentioned only the ones he did."

[*Source*: *Enchiridion* 33]

169. Don't complain
if you don't get what you expect

When you seek to meet with people who are important, remember they may not be available; they may not want to see you or talk to you. If, considering all this, you still want to meet them, by all means go, if it is the right thing to do. But don't complain later that it was not worth it. To do so is the sign of an ordinary person at odds with life.

[*Source*: *Enchiridion* 33]

170. Be restrained in conversations

In conversations, avoid talking at length about yourself. Just because you enjoy your exploits does not mean that others will. They will derive pleasure from hearing about them, not about you.

Avoid trying to be funny.

Avoid using profanities. If someone else uses profanities, and you are sure you are not out of line, you can point it out to the other person. Otherwise, it is enough to show your displeasure by being silent or looking uneasy.

[*Source*: *Enchiridion* 33]

171. Don't let others stop you

When you decide to do something you believe to be right, don't let others stop you, even if a majority of people disapprove of it. If it is a wrong thing to do, you should not do it in the first place. But if it is the right thing, then why care about what others think?

[*Source*: *Enchiridion* 35]

172. Attend to your mind

You should spend some time cultivating the body by eating, drinking, exercising, etc. However, spending too much time cultivating the body at the expense of cultivating the mind shows lack of refinement. While you should take care of your body, you should spend most of your time taking care of your mind.

[*Source*: *Enchiridion* 41]

173. Everything has two handles

Every situation in life comes with two handles: one by which you can carry it and the other by which you cannot. If your brother treats you poorly, the handle, "He harmed me", is the wrong handle to use. Instead, use the other handle, "He is my brother. We grew up together, even if what he does now may look hurtful." It is a better handle to carry the situation.

[*Source*: *Enchiridion* 43]

174. Don't brag about your principles

Don't brag about the principles you follow in life. Don't even mention them to others. Instead, act according to those principles. In social situations, do not tell others how to behave.

If the conversation turns to philosophical principles, keep silent for the most part. Do not be in a hurry to show off what you think you know even before you have digested fully what you learned. If your silence is mistaken for ignorance and you are not upset by it, then it is a real sign of progress.

[*Source*: *Enchiridion* 46]

---

175. Don't advertise your simple life

If you have chosen a simple life, don't make a show of it. If you want to practice simplicity, do so quietly and for yourself, not for others. If you drink only water, don't keep saying on each occasion, *I drink water! Do not embrace stautes!* [Like Cynics used to get used to the coolness of the stone.]

[*Source*: *Enchiridion* 47]

---

176. Be proud of your actions, not of your knowledge

There is no point in being conceited about your ability to understand lofty philosophers. The only thing of importance is to follow the teachings so you can act according to nature. Only when you act according to nature, do you have something to be proud of.

[*Source*: *Enchiridion* 49]

177. Your two guests: body and soul

When you are at a feast, remember you are entertaining two guests – your body and your soul. What you give to your body is soon gone; what you give your soul lasts forever.

[*Source*: Fragments. Schweigh xxxi;
Shenkl *Gen. Epict. Stob*, 20]

178. Don't have more waiters than guests

At meals, see to it that you those who serve be not more in number than those who are served. It is absurd for a crowd of persons to be dancing attendance on half-a-dozen chairs.

[*Source*: Fragments. Schweigh xxiii;
Shenkl *Gen. Epict. Stob*, 23]

179. Be considerate of those who serve you

It is best to share with your attendants, both in labour of preparation and in the enjoyment of the feast itself. If you think that it would be difficult to do so, remember that you who are not tired are being served by those that are; you who are eating and drinking by those who do neither; you who are talking by those who are silent.]; you who are at ease by those who are under constraint. Thus, no sudden anger will lead you to behave unreasonably, nor will you behave harshly by irritating others.

[*Source*: Fragments. Schweigh xxiv;
Shenkl *Gen. Epict. Stob*, 24]

180. Friends wouldn't mind
if we are ourselves

When Xanthippe [wife of Socrates] was chiding Socrates for making scanty preparations for entertaining his friends, he answered: "If they are our friends, they wouldn't care for that; if they aren't, we would care fo them."

[*Source*: Attributed to Epictetus by Maximus;
Schwiegh clxxiii]

181. As long as you are playing,
don't complain

"Who's a rich man?", Someone asked .

"He who is content.", replied Epictetus.

[*Source*: Schwiegh clxxii]

182. Bear and forbear

I have heard Favorinus say this:

The philosopher Epictetus said that most of those who practice philosophy are of the kind 'far from action, only words'. He even used a more vigorous expressions, according to Arrian, who recorded it in his books. Arrian says:

When Epictetus saw someone who lost all sense of shame, whose energy is misguided, who has bad habits, who was disrespectful in speech and who was concerned about everything except their moral character. Epictetus also noticed that such a person was also studying philosophical subjects and methods, physics, and dialectic and was beginning to inquire into many such philosophical ideas. He used to appeal in the name of gods and men, and, in the middle of this appeal, would denounce him with these words:

"Man, where are you putting these things? Look and see if the jar is clean. If you store them among your opinions, they are ruined. If they rot, they become urine or vinegar or perhaps something even worse. Surely, there is nothing more important or truer than this statement: 'The writings and teachings of philosophy, when poured into a false and corrupt person like liquids poured into a dirty and polluted jar, are altered, changed, spoiled and (as he himself in rather Cynic style says) become urine or something even fouler than that."

The same Epictetus, as we have heard from Favorinus, is in the habit of saying that,

"There are two vices much more important and offensive than all the others: lack of self-control and inability to put up with things. We do not put up with and bear things that we should bear and we do not keep away from pleasures and things we should keep away from."

He said:

"So, someone could hold these two words to one's heart and live by them, controlling and keeping watch over themselves, they will, for the most part, be free from wrongdoing and will live a highly peaceful life."

These two words, he used to say, are 'bear' and 'forebear'.

[*Source*: Aulus Gellius xvii, 19. Schweigh clxxix;
Shenkl *Gen. Epict. Stob*, 10]

183. Handy thoughts and prayers

Have these sentiments handy in all circumstances.

"Lead me, Zeus, lead me Destiny
To the goal I was long ago assigned
And I will follow without hesitation.
Even should I resist in a spirit of perversity,
I will have to follow nonetheless."

"Whoever yields to necessity graciously,
We account wise in God's ways."

"Dear Crito, if it pleases gods, so be it."

"Anytus and Meleus can kill me, but they cannot harm me."

[*Source*: *Enchiridion* 53]

184. Handy thoughts and prayers

When we thus follow Socrates, we can spend time writing
hymns in prison.

[*Source*: *Discourses II*.6.16]

185. Face what happens without fear

Blending the two – the carefulness of one devoted to material
things with the stability of one who disregards them – may
appear difficult, but it is not impossible. In fact, it is essential
for our happiness.

Say you are going on a voyage. What can you do?
Whatever is in your power: Pick the captain, the ship, the day,
and the time. Then a storm rises. It's no longer your business,

it's the captain's. You have done everything you could. Now the ship starts to sink. What can you do now? The only thing you can do – sink. But without fear, without crying, and without accusing god; as one who knows what is born must also die. You are not eternal, but a human being. A part of the whole, as an hour is of the day. An hour ends. So does your life.

[*Source*: *Discourses* II.6.16]

186. Externals are nothing to us

We are now sending you to Rome as a spy. But we don't want a coward for a spy – someone who is quick to turn back at the first noise or a glimpse of a shadow, completely frightened and announce, "The enemy is practically among us."

When you return, if you tell us, "Things are dreadful in Rome. Death, exile, poverty, and spies are everywhere. Run you people, the enemy is already among us!" then we will tell you,

"Get lost. And keep your forecasts to yourself. Our only mistake was to send out such a spy."

We had sent Diogenes as a spy and he came back with a very different report. He said, "Death is no evil, because it is not dishonourable. Reputation is the empty noise of fools." He brought great news to remove pain, pleasure, and poverty. He preferred little clothing to purple robes, bare ground to a soft bed. And to prove his claims he produced his courage, tranquillity, and freedom as well as his tough, radiant body.

He said, "There are no enemies nearby! All is profound peace."

[*Source*: *Discourses* I.24, 3-4]

187. Nothing bad can happen to you

When a person has this kind of peace granted to them – not by the government, how can it? – but by God through the voice of reason, isn't he content when he is alone as he thinks and considers this: "Now nothing bad can happen to me; there can be no robbers, no earthquake, and everything is peaceful and tranquil. Every road city, fellow-traveller, neighbour, and associate is harmless. The person who is responsible for food and clothing provides them to me. Another has given me senses and preconceptions. When he stops providing the necessities, he throws open the door and says, 'Go!'"

"Where to?"

"To nothing fearful. Only to that place from which you came. A place that is friendly and akin to you, akin to the elements. Whatever in you was of fire will return to fire; air to air and water to water. There is no underworld or evil spirits. Everything is filled with gods and divine spirits."

If you reflect on this and look upon the sea, moon, and stars and enjoy the earth and sea, you will not be desolate or helpless.

[*Source*: *Discourses* II.13, 12-16]

188. Nothing bad can happen to you

What would you want to be doing when death finds you? As far as I am concerned, I would wish it to be something suitable for a human being, some charitable, public spirited, or noble action. But if I cannot be caught doing anything as great as that, then I should like at least to be doing something that cannot be obstructed and which is proper for me to do: correcting myself, perfecting the faculty that corrects false impressions, and working to achieve calm while fulfilling my social duties. If I am so lucky, advancing to the third division of philosophy dealing with making judgments with confidence.

If death finds me occupied with these things, it is enough for me if I can lift up my hands to God and say,

"I have not neglected the faculties I received from you to understand and follow your rule. I have not dishonoured you, as far as it was in my power. See how I have used my senses and my preconceptions. Have I ever blamed you? Have I ever been dissatisfied with anything that came about, and wished it otherwise? Have I ever violated my social relationships? I am thankful to you for bringing me into this world. I am grateful for the things you have given me. I am content with the length of time I have enjoyed their use. Take them back again and assign them whatever place you wish. They are all yours and you gave them to me."

Isn't it enough to make one's exit in such a state of mind? And what life could be better than this, more fitting than of someone who thinks this way, and what end could be happier?

[*Source*: *Discourses* IV.10, 12-17]

PART 4

The Handbook
(*Enchiridion*)

1. Understand what is in your power and what is not

Some things in life are under your control, and others are not.

What things are under your total control?

What you believe, what you desire or hate, and what you are attracted to or avoid. You have complete control over these, so they are free, not subject to restraint or hindrance. They concern you because they are under your control.

What things are not under your total control?

Your body, property, reputation, status, and the like. Because they are not under your total control they are weak, slavish, subject to restraint, and in the power of others. They do not concern you because they are outside your control.

If you think you can control things over which you have no control, then you will be hindered and disturbed. You will start complaining and become a fault-finding person. But if you deal with only those things under your control, no one can force you to do anything you don't want to do; no one can stop you. You will have no enemy and no harm will come to you.

If you want these substantial rewards in life you should be prepared to put in the effort. This means you may have to give up some things entirely and postpone others for now. If you attempt to get both what is under your control and what is not, you may end up getting neither. Therefore, you need to very clearly distinguish the two.

How do you tell the difference? Start by challenging everything that appears disagreeable. "You are only an appearance. Let me fully understand what you are." Then, using the distinction we talked about, examine it to see if it is under your total control. If it is not within your control, it is nothing to you; there's nothing to worry about.

---

2. Avoid only things under your control

We are ruled by our desires and aversions. When we desire something, we aim to get it. If we don't get what we desire, we feel disappointed.

When we are averse to something, we want to avoid it. If we end up getting what we don't want anyway, we feel unhappy.

If you desire and avoid only those things that are under your control, then you will not feel victimized by things you dislike. But if you resent unavoidable things like illness, misfortune, or death, that are not under your control, you are headed for disappointment.

Instead of showing dislike for what you cannot control, direct your dislike to things that are under your control but are contrary to your nature.

For now, suspend your desires. If you desire something outside your control you are bound to be disappointed. Even when we do control things, the outcome may not be what we desire.

Select carefully what you want to choose and what you want to refuse. Be disciplined and detached while making the choice.

---

3. Remind yourself of the nature of things

When something is delightful or useful to you, remind yourself of its true nature. Start with small things. Suppose you like a ceramic cup you own. Tell yourself, "I love this ceramic cup." Then, if it breaks, you won't be disturbed because ceramic materials tend to break at some point.

Then try this with something that you consider a little more precious.

Eventually extend this understanding to everything. When you kiss your spouse or child, remind yourself that it is a mortal that you are kissing. Then you won't be too distraught should they be taken from you.

4. Remember things can go wrong

Whenever you plan on doing something, mentally rehearse what can happen. If you are headed to a public swimming pool, remember people will splash, push, and yell. They may even steal your things. Or something else may happen to spoil your day. You will be at peace if you tell yourself, "Not only do I need a bath, but I also want to be calm and attuned to nature. Doing so would be impossible if I fell apart whenever something unexpected happened."

5. It's your judgments that disturb you

Events don't disturb people; the way they think about events does. Even death is not frightening by itself. But our view of death, that it is something we should be afraid of, frightens us.

So when we are frustrated, angry or unhappy, let's hold ourselves responsible for these emotions because they are the result of our judgments. No one else is responsible for them.

When you blame others for your negative feelings, you are being ignorant. When you blame yourself for your negative feelings, you are making progress. You are being wise when you stop blaming yourself or others.

6. You are not what you own

Don't be proud of the things you own. We could understand if your horse bragged about its beauty. But, don't you see that when you brag about your horse's beauty, you are taking credit for the horse's traits?

What quality belongs to you? The intelligent understanding of your first impressions. If you analyse your first impressions according to nature (meaning using reason), you will not be puffed with pride unless there is reason for you to be.

7. Always be prepared

When you are travelling by ship, you can go to the shore, enjoy the scenery, collect shells, or pick flowers. But when you are called back to the ship, you need to drop everything and hurry back, otherwise the ship may leave without you.

So it is with life. You have taken many responsibilities: your spouse, your children, and the like. But remember; you must be prepared to give up everything when called back.

8. What will be will be

Don't wish for things to happen the way you would like them to. Rather, welcome whatever happens. This is the path to peace, freedom, and happiness.

9. The mind is not affected by problems

Sickness is a problem for the body, not the mind, unless the mind decides that it is. Similarly, for lameness. It's the body's problem, not the mind's. If you practice attributing the correct source to problems you face, whatever happens, you will soon find that nothing that happens outside of you pertains to you.

10. You have the resources to face any challenge

Remember that for every challenge you face, you have the resources within you to cope with that challenge. If you are inappropriately attracted to someone, you will find you have the resource of self-restraint. When you have pain, you have the resource of endurance. When you are insulted, you have the resource of patience. If you start thinking along these lines, soon you will find that you don't have a single challenge for which you don't have the resource to cope.

11. You can't lose what you don't own

You cannot really lose anything because you don't own anything in the first place. Not the stuff you have, nor your spouse, nor your property. They are given to you for temporary keep. So never say, "I have lost something." You just returned it. Your spouse died? (S)he was returned. You have lost your property? You returned it.

What if a thief stole your things? What does it matter to you who took what doesn't really belong to you? Think of all the things you have as things entrusted to you and you are free to enjoy them for a while. Think of it as a hotel stay. It is checkout time. Leave the hotel behind.

12. Avoid anxious thoughts

If you want to make progress, stop feeling anxious about things. Don't think, "Unless I do such and such a thing, I might end up destitute." Or, "Unless I am strict with my subordinates, they will be undisciplined." Even if these things turn out to be true, it is better for you to be hungry than be anxious. It is better for your subordinates to be undisciplined than for you to be unhappy.

How do you train yourself not to be anxious? Start with small things. For example, you have spilled something on the carpet or something small is stolen from you. Say to yourself, "This is such a small price to pay for tranquillity and peace of mind."

But remember, nothing is free. Things may not work out the way you want. When you choose not to be anxious, you do it in spite of your unfulfilled expectations. What you lose is what you pay for your peace of mind.

---

13. Ignore what others think of you

To make progress, you should be able to accept being seen as ignorant or naïve. Don't strive to be thought of as wise. Even if you succeed in impressing others as a wise person, don't believe it yourself.

You cannot be in agreement with nature and, at the same time, care about things outside your control. Caring about one thing comes at the expense of caring for the other.

---

14. Avoid having unrealistic expectations

You are being foolish if you expect your children, spouse, or friends to live forever. You don't have the power to make this happen.

It is equally naïve to expect everyone will be honest. It is not under your control, but in the control of others who may act honestly or dishonestly. Therefore, we are at the mercy of whomever has control over things we desire or detest.

You can, however, avoid disappointment and be free if you do not desire or avoid things that other people control.

---

15. Be gentle in your dealings

Always conduct yourself as though you are at a formal dinner. If the dish has not reached you yet, don't be impatient. Wait your turn. When it comes around to you, reach out and take a modest amount. If it passes by you, don't try to pull it back.

If you act the same gentle and restrained way with your spouse, children, wealth, and status, you will be entitled to dine with the gods. If you go a step further and decline even what is given to you, you will not only be in the company of gods, but share their powers as well.

---

16. Be compassionate

You may see people who are distraught and in tears because they had to part with their child or lost some material possession. Don't let the impression lead you to think that something bad happened to them. They are not upset by what happened to them but by their view of the situation.

However, be careful not to show disdain for their grief. Show them sympathy, use comforting words, and even share their misery outwardly. But make sure that you do not inwardly grieve with them.

17. Think of yourself as an actor

Consider yourself as an actor in a play. The nature of the play – whether short or long – is for the director to decide. The director will also decide whether your role is one of a poor person, a rich person, a cripple, a king, or a commoner. You as an actor do not decide these things.

Like an accomplished actor you need to perform the role assigned to you in life skilfully. The responsibility for deciding what role you play rests with someone else.

18. Everything is auspicious

If you come across anything you find to be an impediment to your progress – even if it be something you see as an inauspicious sign, something that will bring you bad luck, do not be upset by it. Examine the impression. It is of no significance to you. Nothing outside of you really pertains to you.

For you, every sign is auspicious, if you want it to be that way. Whatever happens, you can derive benefit from it.

19. No reason to envy others

When you confine yourself to only those things that are under your control, you cannot be defeated.

Don't be fooled by outward appearances. People with more prestige, power, or some other distinction are not necessarily happier because of what they have.

There is no reason to be envious or jealous of anyone. If you lead a rational life, the good lies within you. Our concern should be our freedom, not titles and prestigious positions. The way to freedom is not to be too concerned about things we don't control.

20. Don't react impulsively

When someone provokes you, if you respond with anger or some other negative emotion, your mind is tricked into believing you are being harmed. So it is essential not to respond to impressions impulsively. Take some time before reacting. You will see you are in better control.

21. Remember death

Whenever you face difficult situations in life, remember the prospect of death and other major tragedies that can and do happen to people. You will see that, compared to death, none of the things you face in life is important enough to worry about.

22. Be prepared to be laughed at

If you decide to live by lofty principles, be prepared to be laughed at by others. You may hear snide remarks: "Oh, here comes the philosopher!" or "Why are you so pretentious?"

Just ignore those comments. But make sure that you don't become pretentious. If you stick to your principles, people who make fun of you will eventually come around and may even admire you.

However, if you let others influence you to give up what you started, you will be ridiculed twice: firstly, for following these principles, and secondly, for giving them up.

---

23. Don't seek outside approval

You compromise your integrity when you seek outside approval. Be satisfied that you live up to your rational principles. Be your own witness if you need one. You don't need any more witness than that.

---

24. Don't compromise your integrity

Don't let thoughts like, "People won't think well of me," or, "I will live in complete obscurity," bother you. Is living in obscurity bad? Do you decide how you will be recognized and whether you will get the job you deserve? Do you decide whether you will be invited to a party? No, you don't. How can what someone else chooses to do dishonour you?

You may say that unless you get a better job, you won't be able to help your friends. Whoever told you this is your responsibility? Who expects you to give others what you don't have?

If you can make money remaining honest, trustworthy, and dignified, by all means do it. But you don't have to make money if you have to compromise your integrity. A good friend would rather you didn't compromise your integrity than wish you gave him money.

You may then say that your community will be helpless unless you help. Your money can buy only material things for your community. So what? The community will benefit more by the presence of a lawful and loyal member than by material gifts. You cannot be much use to the community if you are shameless and corrupt.

---

25. Everything has a price

Suppose someone else is preferred over you in public and their advice is sought in preference to yours, how should you respond? If he deserves it, you should be pleased for him. If he does not deserve it, don't get upset.

You cannot expect to get the same results he got unless you are prepared to do everything he was prepared to do. If you don't flatter, you will not have the advantages a flatterer will have. Those who are servile to their superiors will be rewarded differently from those who are not.

Everything has a price. For example, let's say that someone pays the retail price to get a head of lettuce. If you decide not to pay the price and go without the lettuce, you are not inferior to that person. He has the lettuce but you still have the money.

It's the same with social situations. If you are not invited to a party maybe it is because you didn't pay the price, such as flattering the host or doing things to be in her good books. So if you want to be invited, pay the bill and don't complain about the cost. But if you expect the benefits without paying the price you are not only greedy, you are being foolish.

What if you are not invited to the party? You did not do things you didn't want to do such as flattering the host. You have the advantage of not compromising your integrity.

26. Apply your wisdom to yourself

When a friend breaks a cup, we are quick to say, "Oh, too bad. But these things happen." But when we break a cup we are easily upset. We need to accept what happens to us in the same spirit as we expect others to accept their lot.

We can apply this understanding to more serious things. When someone else's spouse or child dies, we commonly say, "Well, that's part of life." But when one of our own family members is involved we say, "Poor me. Why did this happen to me?"

Remember how wisely you understand when others face unfortunate situations. Apply the same wisdom when something unfortunate happens to you. Learn to accept whatever happens.

27. Evil is not intentional

No one sets up a target so others can miss it. Similarly, nature has not set up evil in this world so you can avoid it.

28. Let not others control your mind

If your body was turned over to someone else, you would be ashamed and outraged. Should you not be equally ashamed when you turn over your mind to others so they can control it?

Why do you let your mind be controlled by anyone who happens to criticize you? Why do you get confused and upset?

---

29. Look before you leap

When you are about to undertake a project, consider not only what is involved now but what it would involve later. Otherwise you would plunge in enthusiastically at the beginning and end up quitting in disgrace when things get difficult later.

You would like to win at the Olympics? So would I. Who wouldn't? But consider what you need to do now and what you need to do later on before committing to it. You have to submit yourself to rigorous discipline, maintain a strict diet, avoid rich but tasty food, exercise long hours in inclement weather, refrain from drinking alcohol, and give up some of your social life. In short, you should hand yourself over to your trainer.

It's not over yet. There will be times when you will dislocate your wrist, turn your ankle, and swallow sand. After all this, you may still end up losing. If, after considering all this, you still want to get involved, give it a go.

If you don't pause to consider what is involved, you will end up like a child: wrestler one minute, gladiator the next; actor one minute, musician the next. You will be like a monkey that imitates whatever comes its way, drawn by different things. You have not paid attention, and you have not thought things through. You are being casual and arbitrary.

Some people listen to a great philosopher and immediately want to be like him. Find out what you need to do to be a philosopher, just as you would find out what physical attributes you should have to become a pentathlete or a wrestler. Not everyone is cut out to do everything. If you become a philosopher you won't be able to drink and eat in the same way you now do. You may have to stay up late, put up with pain, leave your family, be looked down upon by others, and suffer ridicule from strangers. Are you prepared to pay this price for serenity and freedom? If not, don't go near it. You can't be like a child playing different roles. You have to be one person and stick with the role you have chosen for yourself.

---

30. Keep your side of relationships

Understand your connections to other people. In a relationship, it does not matter what the other person does. This man is your father. Your part of the relationship demands that you respect and support him and even tolerate his erratic behaviour. He may be a bad father, but remember you are entitled only to a father, not to a good father.

Again if you have a brother who is unfair, do not concern yourself with his behaviour, but keep your behaviour in tune with nature.

No one can hurt you unless you let them. You are hurt the moment you believe you are.

In all social dealings – as a father, mother, brother, friend, citizen, etc. – remember what your role is. It does not matter what the other person does.

31. Piety is not separate
from self-interest

If a divine order exists, as it does, we should hold correct beliefs about it. The order governs the world well and is just. We are here to be in tune with the natural order of things and welcome whatever happens as the product of the highest intelligence. This way you will neither blame the divine order nor think that it does not exist.

But first you should stop applying labels like "good" and "bad" to what is not under your control. The labels good and bad apply only to things under your control. If you consider anything beyond your control as good or bad, you will fail to get what you want and get what you don't want. You will blame the divine order and think of it as the cause of your troubles

Everything in nature moves away from whatever is harmful and moves towards whatever is helpful. If you believe that someone has harmed you, you cannot love the offender or the offence. This is the reason why children who don't get what they want blame their parents, farmers curse the weather, and those who have lost their loved ones curse the gods.

Piety does not exist apart from self-interest. Therefore, when you practice using desire and aversion in the right way, you practice being pious.

Even so, it is never wrong to make sacrifice, offer drinks or other things to people, as long as it is done mindfully and not casually. Do not be miserly in your giving but be careful that you do not spend beyond your means either.

32. You don't need to know the future

There is no need to consult astrologers to predict the future. We know that the events over which we have no control can be neither good nor bad. Since the future is not under our control it is nothing to us. Even if you believe in astrologers and consult them to predict the future, remember you are only learning about the future. Your problems can only be solved by reason.

No matter what the predictions for the future are, they do not override your obligations now to your friends, family, and country.

33. Be true to yourself

Decide first what type of person you want to be and stick to it. Be the same person whether you are by yourself or with others. Here are some suggestions:

- Don't indulge in unnecessary chatter. Avoid gossiping about others. Speak with precision and speak about what really matters.
- If you want to influence your friends, do it by your example.
- Do not laugh too loud or too often.
- If possible, avoid taking oaths.
- Avoid fraternizing with people who don't share your values. Prolonged association with those with false ideas can only tarnish your thinking.

- Be moderate in meeting the needs of your body, be it food, drink, clothing, shelter, or household needs. Avoid ostentation and luxury.

- Do not indulge in sexual impropriety. Don't be judgmental of those who do.

- Don't defend yourself if someone speaks ill of you.

- When you go to games, don't side with anyone except yourself. Wish for what happens to happen. Don't keep discussing the game long after it is over.

- When you go to listen to other people's lectures, remain attentive. Don't be disagreeable.

- When you go to meet someone, especially someone important, think of yourself as a dignified person and behave accordingly. You will get on with the other person, no matter what happens.

- When you seek to meet with people who are important, remember they may not be available; they may not want to see you or talk to you. If, considering all this, you still want to meet them, by all means go, if it is the right thing to do. But don't complain later that it was not worth it. To do so is the sign of an ordinary person at odds with life.

- In conversations, avoid talking at length about yourself. Just because you enjoy your exploits does not mean that others will. They will derive pleasure from hearing about them, not about you.

- Avoid trying to be funny.

- Avoid using profanities. If someone else uses profanities, and you are sure you are not out of line, you can point it out to the other person. Otherwise, it is enough to show your displeasure by being silent or looking uneasy.

34. Pause to consider the consequences

When something looks pleasurable, don't get carried away by that impression. Take a minute and let it sink in. Then consider its effect at the time you experience pleasure and later. Will you still be happy or will you regret having indulged in something that's not good for you? Think about how good you would feel if you controlled yourself instead of being swayed by your first impression.

Take extra care to make sure you are not pushed around by the seductiveness of impressions. Think about how much better you will feel if you exercise self-control.

35. Don't let others stop you

When you decide to do something you believe to be right, don't let others stop you, even if a majority of people disapprove of it. If it is a wrong thing to do, you should not do it in the first place. But if it is the right thing, then why care about what others think?

36. Consider the big picture

Statements like, "It's day", and, "It's night", don't tell us what they mean if taken together. Similarly, serving yourself a large portion of healthy food may do good to your body, but would it help communal spirit if you did it at a dinner party? Be considerate of yourself, but also of others.

37. Don't try to do things beyond your means

Don't undertake to do things that are beyond your means. If you do, you will not only embarrass yourself but you will also miss an opportunity to do successful things that are within your means.

38. Care for your mind as much as you care for your body

As you are careful not to step on a sharp object or sprain your ankle, so you should take care not to do any injury to your character. If you exercise caution when you act, you are less likely to damage your character.

39. Understand your need the right way

Your shoe size is decided by the size of your feet. Use the same principle when dealing with other things, so you always understand what is right for your needs. Just as you would feel uncomfortable or even fall down when you use the wrong size shoes, so will you stumble if you exceed your limits in other things. Avoid excesses.

40. Cultivate modesty and self-respect

When girls come of age, they start receiving attention for their looks. As a result, they tend to become preoccupied with their appearances to the exclusion of other things. They should also concern themselves with cultivating modesty and self-respect.

41. Attend to your mind

You should spend some time cultivating the body by eating, drinking, exercising, etc. However, spending too much time cultivating the body at the expense of cultivating the mind shows lack of refinement. While you should take care of your body, you should spend most of your time taking care of your mind.

42. Treat your critics with compassion

When someone criticizes you, they do so because they believe they are right. They can only go by their views, not yours. If their views are wrong, it is they who will suffer the consequences. Keeping this in mind, treat your critics with compassion. When you are tempted to get back at them, remind yourself, "They did what seemed to them to be the right thing to do."

43. Use the right handle

Every situation in life comes with two handles: one by which you can carry it and the other by which you cannot. If your brother treats you poorly, the handle, "He harmed me", is the wrong handle to use. Instead, use the other handle, "He is my brother. We grew up together, even if what he does now may look hurtful." It is a better handle to carry the situation.

44. You are not what you have

Don't say, "I am richer so I am better than you" or, "I am a more persuasive speaker, therefore I am better than you." If you are richer than me, you have more money than me; if you are a more persuasive speaker, you have better persuasive skills. But you are not your wealth, your diction, or any of the things you own.

45. Judge things precisely

If someone bathes quickly, don't say he doesn't bathe properly, say he bathes quickly. If someone drinks a lot, don't say he is a drunk, say he drinks a lot. Unless you know their reasons for their actions how can you be sure of your negative judgment of them? Not judging others too quickly will save you from misperceiving their actions.

46. Don't brag about your principles

Don't brag about the principles you follow in life. Don't even mention them to others. Instead, act according to those principles. In social situations, do not tell others how to behave.

If the conversation turns to philosophical principles, keep silent for the most part. Do not be in a hurry to show off what you think you know even before you have digested fully what you learned. If your silence is mistaken for ignorance and you are not upset by it, then it is a real sign of progress.

Sheep don't bring their owners grass to show how much they ate. Instead, they digest it and produce milk and wool. Similarly, don't make a show of principles you live by. Instead, live by them fully and show others by your actions how much you have learned and made it your own.

---

47. Don't advertise your simple life

If you have chosen a simple life, don't make a show of it. If you want to practice simplicity, do so quietly and for yourself, not for others.

---

48. Help and harm come from you

A wise person understands that help or harm come exclusively from herself. An ordinary person, on the other hand, looks for help or harm from others.

As you make progress, you will stop criticizing, blaming, or flattering others. You will not tell others how much you know or how important you are. If you are frustrated or disappointed, you will know you are responsible for it. If you are praised, you will be more amused than delighted. And you won't respond to criticisms. You will keep in mind you still have a long way to go.

Moreover, you will have no desires that are contrary to nature, and you will know you are in full control of your aversions. You do not care if others think you are naïve or stupid. Your only concern is to keep your focus on yourself, so you don't damage your progress.

49. Your actions are the only things you can be proud of

There is no point in being conceited about your ability to understand lofty philosophers. The only thing of importance is to follow the teachings so you can act according to nature. Only when you act according to nature, do you have something to be proud of.

50. Stand by your decision

Once you undertake to do something, stick with it and treat it as something that should be carried through. Don't pay attention to what people say. It should not influence you in any way.

51. Demand the best of yourself now

How long will you put off demanding the best of yourself? When will you use reason to decide what is best? You now know the principles. You claim to understand them. Then why aren't you putting these principles into practice? What kind of teacher are you waiting for?

You are not a child anymore; you are fully grown. Don't be lazy and give excuse after excuse. If you continue to do this, your lack of progress may be hidden but, in the end, you will have lived a mediocre life.

Decide that you are an adult, and you are going to devote the rest of your life to making progress. Stick closely to what is best. If you are distracted by pleasure or pain, glory or disrepute, realize that the time is now. The game has started and waiting any further is not an option. Win or lose will be decided today. Use reason to meet every challenge.

---

52. Emphasize action over argument

An argument has three parts. For example,

1. You should not lie;
2. Why you should not lie; and
3. Proof for the claim that you should not lie.

So the third part is necessary for the second part which, in turn, is necessary for the first part. Of these three, the first part is the most important because it points to action. But we are often preoccupied with the third part and we continue to lie, and fail to act according to reason.

---

53. Remember these sentiments

Have these sentiments handy in all circumstances.

"Lead me, Zeus, lead me Destiny
To the goal I was long ago assigned
And I will follow without hesitation.
Even should I resist in a spirit of perversity,
I will have to follow nonetheless."

"Whoever yields to necessity graciously,
We account wise in God's ways."

"Dear Crito, if it pleases gods, so be it."

"Anytus and Meleus can kill me, but they cannot harm me."

ABOUT THE AUTHOR

Dr Chuck Chakrapani has been a long-term, but embarrassingly inconsistent, practitioner of Stoicism. He is the president of Leger Analytics, Chief Knowledge Officer of The Blackstone Group in Chicago and a Distinguished Visiting Professor at Ryerson University.

Chuck has written books on several subjects over the years which include research methods, statistics, and investment strategies. His personal website is ChuckChakrapani.com

His books on Stoicism include *Unshakable Freedom, A Fortunate Storm* and *The Good Life Handbook* (a rendering of Epictetus' *Enchiridion*.)

Also by the Author

Stoic Foundations

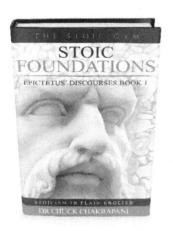

Stoic Foundations is the plain English version of Discourses Book 1 by the eminent Stoic philosopher Epictetus.

It revolves around 10 themes which are also repeated in other places throughout Discourses. These are:

- Concern yourself with only what is in your power
- Be content to let things happen as they do
- Your thinking, not the externals, drives your behaviour
- Do not place value on external things
- Don't give in to your anger or animal instincts
- You can handle anything; always act your best Learn to think properly and logically
- Practice, not knowledge, results in progress
- Only you can make you happy

Available from your favourite online bookstore.

Stoic Choices

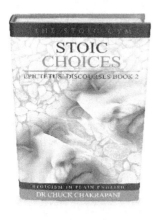

Stoic Choices is the plain English version of Discourses Book 2 by the eminent Stoic philosopher Epictetus.

It revolves around 10 themes which are also repeated in other places throughout Discourses. Here are some of the choices discussed in this book:

• What should you act upon: External things or internal things?

• When should you choose to be confident and when to be cautious in making decisions?

• What should you protect: Your inherent qualities or qualities that are not inherent to you?

• Is there a choice between knowledge and action?

• Is there a choice between knowledge and anxiety?

• Should you study logic? Why?

• Choose to be faithful.

• Choose habits that fight impressions.

• Show yourself to be worthy.

• Choose to be skilful.

Available from your favourite online bookstore

Stoic Training

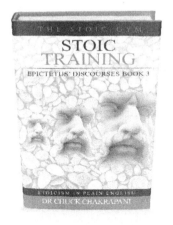

This is the third book of *Discourses* of Epictetus in plain English. Stoics did not believe in just theoretical knowledge but held that it is critical we practice what we learned. Here are the basic themes of Stoic training explored by Epictetus here:

- Stoic training aims to make you excellent as a human being.
- Stoic training consists of three disciplines: desire, action and assent.
- Stoic training consists only of dealing with one's choices.
- Train you mind to want whatever actually happens.
- Stoic training means to prepare ourselves for the challenges to come.
- Ascetic training is unnecessary unless it serves some purpose.
- Train to see things as they are without adding your judgements to them.
- Your judgements are the sole cause of your distress, because nothing outside of you can harm you.
- Don't imitate others without understanding the basis of their actions.]
- Train to be at home wherever you are. Things are impermanent.
- Your goal is happiness and good fortune.

Stoic Freedom

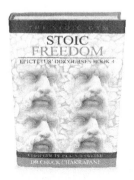

This is the fourth book of Discourses of Epictetus in plain English. Personal freedom is close to Epictetus' heart and his rhetoric shines when he talks about freedom. This is what he has to say about achieving personal freedom that is robust and unshakable:

- Your desires imprison you. If you confine your desire only to what is under your control, then you will never be unfree.
- Freedom has a price. If you want to be free, be prepared to pay
- The more value you attach to external things, the less free you are to choose.

But what does a free person look like?

- A free person is not in conflict with anyone.
- A free person is patient.
- A free person is not envious.
- A free person is not anxious.
- A free person is pure.
- A free person is steadfast.
- A free person chooses what to reveal about themselves and when..

A Fortunate Storm

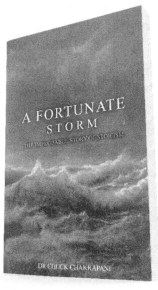

Unshakable Freedom is based on Stoic teachings.

But how did Stoicism come about?

Three unconnected events – a shipwreck in Piraeus, a play in Thebes, and the banishment of a rebel in Turkey – connected three unrelated individuals to give birth to a philosophy. It was to endure two thousand years and offer hope and comfort to hundreds of thousands of people along the way.

The Fortunate Storm is the improbable story of how Stoicism came about. You can get a FREE COPY of the e-version of this book at the link below:

http://www.TheStoicGym.com/fortunatestormfree

The Good Life Handbook

Available in Print, digital, and audio editions.

The Good Life Handbook is a rendering of *Enchiridion* in plain English. It is a concise summary of the teachings of Epictetus, as transcribed and later summarized by his student Flavius Arrian.

The Handbook is a guide to the good life. It answers the question, "How can we be good and live free and happy, no matter what else is happening around us?"

Ancient Stoics lived in a time of turmoil under difficult conditions. So, the solutions they found to living free was tested under very stringent conditions. For example, the author of this Handbook was a lame slave who made himself free and happy later in life by following the principles set out in this book.

Now The Stoic Gym offers *The Good Life Handbook* by Dr Chuck Chakrapani to interested readers free (Kindle and other online versions).

Please get your copy in your favourite online bookstore.

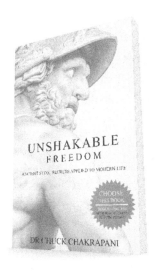

How can we achieve total personal freedom when we have so many obligations and so many demands on our time? Is personal freedom even possible?

Yes, it is possible, said the Stoics and gave us a blue print for freedom. The teachings were lost but have been rediscovered in recent times and form the basis of modern cognitive therapy.

In his new book, *Unshakable Freedom*, Dr Chuck Chakrapani outlines the Stoic secrets for achieving total freedom, no matter who you are and what obstacles you face in life.

Using modern examples, Chuck explores how anyone can achieve personal freedom by practicing a few mind-training techniques

Made in the USA
Coppell, TX
28 January 2022